DORSET

Place Names

DORSET

Place Names

Anthony Poulton-Smith

AMBERLEY

First published 2010

Amberley Publishing
Cirencester Road, Chalford,
Stroud, Gloucestershire, GL6 8PE

www.amberley-books.com

British Library Cataloguing in Publication Data.
A catalogue record for this book is available from the British Library.

ISBN 978 1 84868 726 4

Typesetting and origination by Amberley Publishing
Printed in Great Britain

Contents

Introduction

For years the history of England was based on the Roman occupation. In recent years, we have come to realise the influence of the Empire did not completely rewrite British history, indeed there was already a thriving culture in England well before the birth of Christ. When the Romans left our shores in the fifth century, the arrival of the Anglo-Saxons was thought to herald a time of turmoil, yet they brought the culture and language that forms the basis of modern England. The same is true of our place names, the vast majority of settlement names in Dorset are derived from this Saxon or Old English language, while the topographical features, such as rivers and hills, still have names given to them by the Celts of the pre-Roman era.

Ostensibly place names are simply descriptions of the location, uses and people who lived there. In the pages that follow, an examination of the origins and meanings of the names in Dorset will reveal all. Not only will we see Saxons settlements, but Celtic rivers, Roman roads, and even Norman French landlords who have all contributed to the evolution to some degree of the names we are otherwise so familiar with.

Not only are the basic names discussed but also districts, hills, streams, fields, roads, lanes, streets, and public houses. Road and street names are normally of more recent derivation, named after those who played a significant role in the development of a town or revealing what existed in the village before the developers moved in. The benefactors who provided housing and employment in the eighteenth and nineteenth centuries are often forgotten, yet their names live on in the name found on the sign at the end of the street and often have a story to tell. Pub names are almost a language of their own. Again, they are not named arbitrarily but are based on the history of the place and can open a new window on the history of our towns and villages.

With any story or narrative for it to be seen as a good story it is essential to make the reader feel a part of the scene. In the author's opinion, the same is true of place names and the best place names are those which describe the scene and produce a virtual snapshot of life in Anglo-Saxon England and one which would otherwise be lost forever. Defining place names of all varieties can give an insight into history which would otherwise be ignored or even lost. In the ensuing pages we shall examine 2,000 plus years of Dorset history. While driving around this area, the author was delighted by the quintisentially English place names and so, having already taken a look at Oxfordshire Place Names, Hampshire Place Names, Gloucestershire Place Names, North Devon Place Names and South Devon Place Names, turned to Dorset. This book is the result of the author's long interest in place names, which has developed over many years and is the latest in a series that continues to intrigue and surprise.

To all who helped in my research, from the librarians who produced the written word to those who pointed a lost traveller in the right direction, those who provided a comfortable bed, a welcome meal, and who quenched my thirst, a big thank you.

The hamlet of Nether Cerne.

Chapter 1

Abbotsbury to Athelhampton

ABBOTSBURY

From the Old English *abbod burh* comes 'the fortified house or manor of the abbot', a reference to its possession by the abbot of Glastonbury. The name was listed as Abbedesburie in 946 and Abedesberies 1086.

The Swan Inn can have a number of meanings; however, here there is no sizable river on which the bird is always depicted, hence this is not the source. Thus it must be heraldic and, while there is no colour, as we would normally expect, can probably be traced back to the royal house of Henry VIII or earlier still to Edward III.

ADBER

Recorded as Eatan in 956 and as Ateberie in 1086, this features a personal name with Old English bearu, thus telling us this was 'the grove of a man called Eata'.

AFFPUDDLE

In 1086, this name is recorded as Affapidele, an Old English name from 'the farmstead on the River Piddle of a man called Aeffa'. The river name is discussed under its own heading.

This parish also has a Bryants Puddle, here there are several additions recorded, all of whom are members of the same family of de Turbervill, the gentleman seen in today's name is that of Brian de Turbervill who was here in 1316. Throop is an interesting and rarely seen form of thorp, an Old English term for an 'outlying or secondary settlement'. Dead Woman's Stone is certainly a boundary marker, although whether it marks the death or last resting place of anyone is unknown.

ALDERHOLT

Listed as Alreholt in 1285, this is an Old English name from *alor holt* and describing the '[place at] the alder wood'.

Crendell comes from *crundel* meaning 'a pit, quarry'; Daggons Farm takes the name of the family of Richard Dagon, here by 1327; Perry Copse and Perry Farm share a common origin in *pyrige* or 'at the pear trees'; Bartley Wood and Bartley Row is derived from Old English *beorc leah* and *beorc raw* respectively, the names meaning 'the woodland clearing near the birch trees' and the 'birch tree row'. Cheater's Lane gets its name from the family of William Chatere, who were here by 1530. Cripplestyle is from crypel stigel and tells us of 'the stile that could be crept through (by sheep)'. Minnows Hole takes its name from the pool near the ford 'the hole where minnows are found'. Stanford Point was the home to Richard de Stanford, who was here by 1283. Wolvercroft is either 'the small enclosed field of a man called Wulfhere', or possibly from *wulf* and describing where this animal was known to have a den on a regular basis.

The Churchill Arms has been renamed, earlier being the Railway Arms and a reference to Daggons Road Station such to mark former lord of the manor George Churchill. It was Churchill who commented on Alderholt standing almost at the point where three counties meet, and thus one could flush a duck in Dorset, shoot it in Hampshire, and bag it in Wiltshire. Whether this be factual or not, this surely suggests a change of name to the Churchill Duck.

ALLINGTON

A name found as Adelingtone in 1086 and Athelington in 1227, this features a Saxon personal name and Old English *ing tun* and describes 'the farmstead associated with a man called Athelheah'.

ALLWESTON

A name found in 1214 as Alfeston, here the suffix is the common *tun* and means 'the farmstead of a woman called Aelflaed or Alfgifu', but it is not often names are found where women have given their names to a place.

ALMER

The only early record of note dates from 943 as Elmere. Undoubtedly this is Old English *ael mere*, telling us of 'the eel pool'.

Locally we find Mapperton Farm, a name from Old English *mapuldor tun* and refers to 'the farmstead of or by the maple trees'; Great Coll Wood and Coll Wood Cottages show this to come from *col wudu* or 'the wood where charcoal was burnt'; and Parliament House stood at the meeting point of the boundary of three parishes.

The local is the World's End, a name that was used to describe an isloated inn.

ALTON PANCRAS

The basic name of Alton is found all over England, and with a number of different origins. Here it is Old English *aeweill-tun* or 'the farmstead at the source of a river', with the addition telling of the dedication of the Church of St Pancras.

Minterne Parva footpath sign.

ALUM CHINE

Large quantites of alum were mined here from at least the sixteenth century, although this place name is not found until the eighteenth century. It does indeed refer to the mining of alum, a substance used in the processes of making paper and tanning leather.

ANDERSON

A place name recorded as Wintreburne in 1086, the name describes 'the strong winter stream' and is also seen in other Winterbornes nearby. This name persisted until the fifteenth century, when it was also known as Fifassch or Fyfhasche and telling of the '(place of) five ash trees'. Both of these are found to have overlapped with the modern form — an unusual name to evolve from the dedication of the Church of St Andrew.

Local place names include Goschen, from Old English *gaers tun*, or 'the farmstead with a paddock'.

ANSTY CROSS

The basic name here is from Old English *anstig* meaning 'the narrow or lonely track' and one that is also seen as 'track linking with other routes'. Clearly, this is an important

The crossroads at Gallows Hill.

pointer to ancient routes and a name that is common enough to warrant an addition speaking either of the route marker that may have stood here, or of the crossroads formed by the roads themselves. The earliest record on hand is as Anesty in 1219.

ARNE

The modern form is exactly the same as that found in the thirteenth century, and it has two potential Old English beginnings. Either this is *aern*, 'the house or building', or haer, the '(place at) the heaps of stones'.

Minor names here include Slepe, from *slaep* and meaning 'a slippery muddy place'; Stoborough, which means '(there is) a stony barrow (here)'; the odd name of Worgret seems to be from Old English *wearg rod* or 'the gallows', which would have delivered the message on the busy road between Wareham and Dorchester, and there is also a Gallows Hill where the road to Corfe Castle meets the Wareham Road.

Salterns Copse was a place where salt was made and/or sold, and there are a number of records showing that salt was an important commodity here. There were a number of saltings in the area, including one hide here given over to salt production, which was held by twenty tenants of Shaftesbury, with at least one salt pan each. Here salt water was heated in a salt pan until it crystallised out to form the vital ingredient necessary to preserve meat, while much was also used in the tanning of leather and in cloth making.

ASHMORE

Domesday's record of Aisemare points to Old English *aesc mere* meaning of 'the pool where ash trees grow'.

Ashey Knapp is from Old English *aescen cnaepp* and describes 'the hill top growing with ash trees'. Bald Coppice is named from 'the rounded hill', Bench Coppice is that growing on 'the ledge or shelf', Crabtree Coppice is 'where crab apples grow', Wagbush Coppice refers to 'the bush coppice associated with the Wagg family, the family of William Lambert were associated with Lambert's Coppice in the seventeenth century, Washers Pit Coppice points to where washing was regularly seen (and not simply laundry but animal hides, etc), and Sedge Oak Coppice is a corruption of *scid ac* and describing 'the oak plank or beam', which presumably was used as a rudimentary bridge.

ASKERSWELL

Found in 1086 as Scherwille, this name comes from the Old English suffix *wella* and speaks of '(place at) Osgar's stream'.

The local here is the Spyway, the name coming from it said to have been the lookout point used by smugglers.

ATHELHAMPTON

There are two records of Athelhampton of note: Pidele, 1086, and Pidele Athelmaston, 1285. Clearly, this thirteenth century record is the earliest that features the modern name, as prior to this it was named after the River Piddle. Today, the name refers to 'the farmstead of a man called Aethelhelm'.

Chapter 2

Batcombe to Burton Bradstock

BATCOMBE

Recorded as Batecumbe in 1201, this features a personal name with Old English *cumb*, thus telling us this was 'the valley of a man called Bata'.

BEAMINSTER

From a Saxon personal name plus the Old English *mynster* comes 'the large church of a woman called Bebbe' — a rare occasion when a female name is used. The name was listed as Bebingmynster in 862 and Beiminstre in 1086.

Here we find the Knapp, a public house taking the name already marked on the map here. Standing at 'the small hill' it comes from Old English *cnaep* and is usually found as Knap, which strongly suggests the error was on the map when the original owners were looking for a name for their pub. We also find the Greyhound Inn, an animal that was once also called the gazehound for it hunts by sight and not smell. Here the name is probably heraldic, referring to the Dukes of Newcastle who held lands in Dorset.

BEER HACKETT

In 1176, this name is recorded as simply Bera, the addition is not seen until 1362 as Berehaket. This is an Old English name from either *bearu*, 'the grove', or baer, 'the woodland pasture', with the addition coming from the manor being owned by a man named Haket and from at least the twelfth century.

Local names include Knighton, or 'the farmstead of the thegns or knights', which probably refers to the Knights Hospitallers who held land around here; Tibble's Lane is a shortened form of *tadde bola lane* and suggests this was 'the bowl-shaped hollow frequented by toads'; and both Trill Farm and Trill House takes the name of a tributary of the River Yeo, now unnamed it comes from *tyrl* and describes 'that which rolls along'.

BERE REGIS

Despite the different spelling, the basic place name here does indeed come from the same source as the previous name. Hence this is Old English *baeru* or *baer* meaning 'grove' or 'woodland pasture', but here the manor was the property of the Crown, for Latin *regis* means 'of the king'. Listed as simply Bere in Domesday, the addition is not seen until 1264 as Kyngesbyre.

Around this town are a number of names of note, including Chamberlayne's Farm, which reminds us that this place was worked by John Chaumberlayn from at least 1327. Doddings Farm may well come from Middle English *dodde* and describe the 'rounded hill', in which case the *ing* has no relevance, while if the first element is a personal name then this is the '(place) associated with a man called Dodda'. Higher Hove Wood and Lower Hove Wood share a common origin in Old English *hufe* and describe 'the hood shaped hill'.

Philliols Coppice takes the name of the Filiol family, and Hugh and William Filiol are recorded as being here in 1354. Roke Farm gets its name from Middle English *atter oke* or 'the place at the oak tree, the loss of the first syllable is commonplace. Snatford is from Old English *snad ford* and refers to the 'river crossing at the detached piece of woodland'. Higher Stockely Farm and Lower Stockley Farm share a common origin in *stocc leah*, or 'the clearing where stumps remain'. Bugbarrow comes from Old English *bugge beorg* referring to 'the barrow where a hobgoblin is seen'.

A place name that is derived from Old English *scitere tun*, or 'the farm at the stream called Shitter', refers to the fact this watercourse was used as a sewer. While maps will give this as Shitterton, directories and road signs omit the 'h' and point to Sitterton.

The Dungeon is the darkest, thickest part of Bere Wood; Lockyer's Hill was home to Martin Lockeir in 1664; Newfoundland is a remoteness name, a plantation in the extreme south of this parish; Pickard's Coppice is named after the lords of Bloxworth in the seventeenth century, the Pickard family; Spear's Lane was home to Edith Spere in 1586; and Yearlings Bottom and Yearlings Drove probably stem from from *ere*, 'the strips used for ploughing', as for these pieces of land to be grazed only by yearlings seems highly improbable.

Locally we find the Drax Arms; the Drax family came to the estate in the eighteenth century and are still here today. Others drink in the Royal Oak, named after the famous Boscobel Oak in Shifnal, Shropshire, where Charles II and his aide Colonel Carless hid from the Parliamentary soldiers. Fleeing following defeat at the Battle of Worcester in 1651, they hid in its branches for much of the day before being smuggled out of the country into hiding on the Continent; they returning at the Restoration of the Monarchy. The king's birthday was declared Royal Oak Day to commemorate the famous story of the oak tree. Indeed, it is as much the symbolism of the oak tree and the heroic narrative, which has led to it being the second most common pub name in England.

BETTISCOMBE

Found as Bethescomme in 1129, this is the earliest known record of a name that tells us of 'the valley of a man called Betti'. Here the Saxon personal name is followed by the Old English *cumb*, a common element in the southwest of England.

Road sign at Bincombe.

BEXINGTON

Listed as Bessinton in the Domesday Book of 1086, this is an Old English place name derived from *byzen-tun* and meaning 'the farmstead where the box trees grow'.

BINCOMBE

A name found in 987 as Beuncumbe and as Beincome in 1086. This is almost certainly from the Old English *bean-cumb* and tells us it was 'the valley where beans are grown', but it just might represent a personal name.

BLANDFORD FORUM

Records of this name start with Domesday's Blaneford, while the addition is not seen until 1297 as Blaneford Forum. This probably from the Old English *blaege-ford*, or 'the ford where blay are found', and features a word which is now obsolete. Blay is a dialect word for the gudgeon, although it is not always confined to this part of the country, cropping up in the east, the Midlands, and even as far north as Shropshire and Cheshire. It is, of course, quite possible that this term was taken to these parts by those who settled from the south, although the reverse may be the case and this is where the term hung

17

Beres Yard, Blandford Forum, takes visitors to the local museum.

on when it had died out elsewhere. The addition is Latin forum meaning 'market' and is to differentiate from the following name.

Street names here tell their own stories. Damory Street is from the possessions here by the abbey of St Mary in Fintevrault, France. Plocks is often found in towns where there has been minimal change to the layout of the streets; it stems from plock and tells us it lies on 'a small plot of ground'. St Leonard's chapel was recorded as a ruin in 1861, when it was in use as a barn, the place was used to house the leper colony mentioned as being here in the late thirteenth century.

Public houses here include the Dolphin, a symbol associated with many coats of arms and found in the names of ships and families, and indeed it is so common that it is difficult to tell where the name came from.

BLANDFORD ST MARY

As with the previous name this is 'the ford where the bray or gudgeon are found', with the addition a reference to the dedication of the church. This place is also listed as Blaneford in Domesday and as Blandford St Mary in 1254. These fish would have been swimming in the local river, which also gave a name to the Stour Inn.

Local names include Thorncombe Farm, a name that can still be seen as coming from Old English *thorn cumb* or 'the valley where the thorn bushes grow'. The oddly named B Plantation is not an alphabetical reference, but describes the shape of the area as resembling this letter. Lady Caroline's Drive recalls Lady Caroline Damer, a former resident here who died in 1775. Maggot Clump is nothing to do with insect larvae, this is from Old English *maggot* meaning 'mapgie'.

BLOXWORTH

Found in 987 as Blacewyrthe and as Blocheshorde in 1086, this is from a Saxon personal name followed by Old English *worth* and tells us of 'the enclosure of a man called Blocc'.

The term *worth* meaning enclosure is often mistakenly seen as referring to a defensive pallisade of wooden posts behind one or more ditches. This is not strictly accurate, the name refers to something designed to keep livestock in, rather than raiding parties out. At night it made sense to keep the livestock penned in whenever possible to prevent them from roaming, remember the fields of Saxon days were not enclosed as are the modern area. Hence under the cover of darkness they would be able to roam, unseen by the watching eyes of the herdsman.

Here we find the Knoll, a common name from *cnoll* or 'hillock'; Stroud Bridge takes its name from *strod*, or the 'marshy land overgrown with brushwood'; Great Adbury and Little Adbury appear to have taken the name of the family of Joan atte Bergh, who was here by 1327; Botany Bay Barn is a remoteness name, the region being at a northerly corner of the parish; Half Moon is the name of two coppices that together form this shape; Derham's Coppice refers to the family of John Derrome or Matthew Dearam, both of whom were here in 1664; this same year Alexander Humber was associated with Humber's Coppice and Humber's Leg; while James's Coppice seems to have been known as Samuel James's Coppice in 1845 and, while there is no other record of this gentleman, is likely to be the origin of the name.

Sticklehill is from Old English *sticca hyll* and describing 'the hill where sticks are obtained', presumably for fencing or similar small scale building work; Sugar Hill is found on a stretch of the road from Bere to Wareham, likely from Old English *sceacere* meaning 'a robber' and probably a reference to a miserly person or one of dubious character rather than a felon.

BOSCOMBE

With the earliest record coming from 1273 as Boscumbe, this name is derived from Old English *bors-cumb* and describes 'the valley overgrown with spiky plants'.

BOTHENHAMPTON

A name without any surviving record before 1268, where the name is Bothehamton and little different to the modern form. It seems this is from Old English *bothm-ham-tun*, or 'the home farm in the valley'.

BOURNEMOUTH

This popular resort has a name, which, with a little thought, still reveals its origins today. Not recorded before 1407, this name is derived from Old English *burna-mutha*, or the '(place at) the mouth of the stream'.

Local pubs here include the Pig & Whistle, which is not as popular a pub name as one would think. There is no reason for the development of this pub name, it seems the only early record is its use as a generic name for a pub (much as the vacuum cleaner is referred to as a hoover irrespective of its manufacturer). This is thought to have originated from the name the crew have to their bar aboard a merchant vessel. The

The shoreline at Boscombe.

Punch and Judy reminds us that this popular resort will have entertained children for generations with this traditional puppet show, itself originating in Italy and brought here in the seventeenth century.

The Spyglass & Kettle is a created name, taken from two former pubs, known as the Lord Nelson and the Steam Engine, which suggests that the famous admiral was standing on the footplate of a locomotive. Gulliver's might allude to the famous story by Jonathan Swift, but this surname is well documented throughout the county. The Hop and Kilderkin features the crop famously used in brewing with an unusual barrel size from the Netherlands and not often used in this country.

Mary Shelley is named after the woman who is best known for her Gothic novel Frankenstein; or the Modern Promethueus. She was married to poet Percy Bysshe Shelley; however, the pub in Bournemouth is the Sir Percy Florence Shelley, son of the two wordsmiths and whose middle name shows he was born in Florence, Italy. The Athelstan (which should be Aethelstan) was named after the Saxon king of England who reigned 924-35 AD and who was the grandson of the first king of a united England, Alfred the Great.

BOURTON

Bourton is a common place name found throughout England and one which almost always comes from 'the fortified farmstead', *burh tun*, which is indeed the case here. The place is recorded as Bureton in 1212.

Minor names here include Chaffeymoor, which is given to a farm, grange, hill, and house. This name is a particular favourite of the author, for defining it gives such a good description that it provides a snapshot of this place during the Saxon era 1,500 years ago. There are three elements here, *ceaf ieg mor*, and dealing with these in reverse order the last clearly points to the 'moor, heathland' and is a comparatively recent addition; *ieg* is used to describe 'dry land in a marsh or wetland'; and *ceaf* or 'chaff' describes 'rubbish, fallen twigs, debris'. Together this is seen as pointing to the area between the two streams where branches and leaf litter were washed down, a place known as Chaffey well before the addition of moor extended its use.

Sandway is easy to see as 'the sandy way', it points to the road to Zeals where there has been a sand pit marked for many years. Brickyard Lane reminds us of the Brick, Pipe & Tile Works here by 1839; similarly Forge Lane shows the location of the old smithy; Tan Lane almost certainly shows where the tannery was found, and this processing of leather producing a truly obnoxious aroma.

King's Green Cottage has nothing to do with royalty, but is named after Mathew Kinge, whose family were here by 1609, the same year as Marvin's Farm was home to Thomas Marvine's family. Forty Pond is a corruption of forth *ieg* and seen as 'the crossing to the dry land in a marsh'.

BOVINGTON

Here a Saxon personal name is followed by the Old English elements *ing tun* and speaking of 'the farmstead associated with a man called Bofa'. The earliest record is from 1086 as Bovintone.

BRADFORD ABBAS

The addition should be expected, for this is one of the most commonly found place names in England. Indeed, it is no wonder this is so common, for 'the broad ford' would have been a popular and important crossing point of any stream in a region. Coming from Old English *brad ford* it is not (as is sometimes suggested) the breadth of the river but that of the ford — that is, the stream is crossable for more than just the width of a single cart at this point. This name is recorded as Bradanforda in 933, as Bradeford in 1086, and as Braddefor Abbatis in 1386, where the distinctive addition is from the Latin *abbas* or 'abbot' and refers to this manor being under the control of Sherbourne Abbey.

Babylon Hill seems to have taken its name from a local name for the road which connected Yeovil with other important places such as Sherborne, Salisbury, and eventually London, and indeed the English capital city was probably suggested as being Babylon, for that term was used to describe any great city of high living for many years.

BRADFORD PEVERELL

As if to prove how common the 'broad ford' name really is, here is another Old English *brad ford* and is found as Bradeford in Domesday and Bradeford Peuerel in 1244. Here the addition refers to the Peverel family, who were known to be here by the thirteenth century.

The local reference to Muckleford is derived from 'Mucel or Mucela's ford', while the name of Seven Barrow Plantation may be obvious but all signs of the tumuli disappeared under the plough and cultivation many years ago.

BRADPOLE

Found in Domesday as Bratepolie, this eleventh-century record shows the origins to be Old English *brad pol* or 'the broad pool'.

BRANKSOME

A modern name, Branksome was created in 1855 when the house known as Branksome Tower was built. The place name certainly did not occur before this and is thought to have been taken from a novel by Sir Walter Scott entitled Lay of the Last Minstrel, first published in 1805.

Alderney Heath comes from Old English *alren* meaning 'where alders grow'; Coy Pond is an abbreviation of 'decoy', probably to fool or capture poachers; and the name Rossmore is from Celtic *ros* and Old English *mor*, both referring to 'moorland'.

BRIANTSPUDDLE

This name is found in 1086 as simply Pidele, the name of the River Piddle (discussed under its own heading) is the basis for this name. Later, the name becomes Brianis Pedille, as seen in a record of 1465, which shows that during the fourteenth century the lord of the manor was a man called Brian.

BRIDE (RIVER)

A Celtic river name, Bride perfectly described this fast-flowing river as 'the gushing or surging stream'.

BRIDPORT

Recorded in Domesday as Brideport, this name also takes its name from the River Bride, but not directly for this is not the River Bride but the Brit. In order to understand this we have to realise the origins of the place name, particularly that of the Old English *port*, which in Saxon times meant 'a market' and not just a harbour. Thus the place name should be seen as 'the market town belonging to Bredy' and referring to Long Bredy, which, as already stated, takes its name from the River Bride.

Here the river is called the Brit, which can only have come from the place and is thus one of those cases referred to as back-formation. It seems likely there was an earlier name for this river but no record of this has ever been found. However, this is not confined to ancient names, as is seen in the following example.

The link to the sea is seen in the names of the three local pubs. The Ropemakers was a skill that required co-operation between several men, and a long area in which to plait and entwine the rope fibres, many miles of which were required on sailing ships. Onboard a ship the quarter-deck is traditionally that upper part aft of the mainsail and reserved for officers, passengers and guests, thus the Quarter Deck Tavern offers a welcome to the more important of those on board. The Loders Arms takes its name from the small settlement discussed under its own entry, and most likely brought here as a surname.

BROADMAYNE

Domesday shows this as simply Maine, which by 1202 had become Brademane. This features two elements, the earliest is Celtic main and speaking of 'a rock or stone', which later joined by Old English *brad*, which means 'broad' but could also be seen as great. Just where this stone is today and, if it was not a boundary marker, what was significant about it is unknown.

Here we see the name of Poor Lot, which does not mean a region of substandard soil. Indeed, Poor Lot means quite the reverse, for it was left by a landowner to the church in order to raise money for the poor of the parish.

BROADSTONE

As seen in the previous name, this is a name referring to 'a broad stone'. However, unlike the previous name, this is a very recent name, given to a parish formed in 1905.

BROADWEY

A name recorded in 1086 as simply Waia and in 1243 as Brode Way. This name undoubtedly comes from the River Wey, which is discussed under its own heading, to which the Old English *brad* was added by the thirteenth century. On the face of it this means 'the broad Wey', yet it is also possible this refers to the 'the broad estate on the Wey'.

Local names include Nottington, or 'the farmstead associated with a man called Hnotta'; Coffin Plantation is nothing sinister, it comes from a common seventeenth-century surname; Jones's Hole is a corruption of 'John's or Joan's hollow'; Lorton refers to itself as 'the dirty or muddy farmstead'; while Watery Lane follows part of the course of the River Wey.

St Hubert's Church, Broadstone.

The Willett Arms, Broadstone.

BROADWINDSOR

Recorded in 1086 as Windesore and as Brodewyndesore in 1324, this name is of Old English origin in *windels ora* and speaking of 'the river bank with a windlass'. This would have been used to winch goods unloaded from the river up the slippery bank to the settlement.

The local is the White Lion, which, as with all coloured animals, is a pub name of heraldic origins. As with many such images, it is often difficult to understand which figure it was intended to represent, but the majority point to either Edward IV, the earls of March, or the dukes of Norfolk.

BROWNSEA ISLAND

Not found until Brunkeseye in 1241, this name features the Old English *eg* and speaks of 'the island of a man called Brunoc'. This island in Poole Harbour must have attracted potential residents from early times, although it would always have relied on goods brought in to sustain any population.

BRYANSTON

Listed in 1268 as both Blaneford Brian and also Brianeston, this name comes from the Old English for 'Brian's farmstead'. In the thirteenth century, this name was recorded as being held by Brian de Insula. It should also be noted that this name could well have evolved as Blandford Brian, for originally this place was called Blandford (see Blandford Forum and Blandford St Mary).

The Cliff Linhay features the Dorset dialect linhay, or 'lean-to shed'; its location near the cliff is evident, as is the place name of the Bushes Linhay. Fair Mile Plantation lies alongside Fair Mile Road, which is somewhat of a misnomer for it refers to a stretch of straight road running for a little over one and a half miles. However, the name Shothole is accurate, for this was where a small hole in a fortified wall really did allow someone to shoot when well hidden. Doubtless this refers to the hide of hunting station.

BUCKHORN WESTON

Old English *west tun*, which does mean 'the western farmstead', is clearly named by those east of here and indeed quite possibly an offshoot of this settlement. This is so common as a place name that additions are to be expected, and here it refers to the manor being owned by someone called Bowker in medieval times. The name is recorded as Westone in Domesday and Boukeresweston in 1275.

Abbey Ford Bridge shows how this was formerly a possession of the Abbess of Shaftesbury, together with adjoining parishes across the border in Somerset. Caggypole Farm takes the dialect term *caggy* that comes from Old English cag meaning 'clog, surfeit' and together with *pol* suggests the 'stagnant pool, one choked with vegetation', which is close to Filley Brook —another name describing 'the foul or dirty brook'. Gigg

Lane was one regularly used by a gig, a light two-wheeled carriage pulled by a single horse. The Stapleton Arms Inn is one of the few surviving reminders of the name of the lords of the manor from the nineteenth century.

BUCKLAND NEWTON

A name recorded as Boclonde in 941, as Bochelande in 1086, and Newton Buckland in 1576. The basic name here is Old English *boc land* meaning 'the charter land', that is an estate which by royal decree in Saxon times has acquired certain rights and privileges. Normally the addition here would be Old English *niew tun* 'the new farmstead', but here this addition is to differentiate from other Bucklands in neighbouring Devon and is taken from Sturminster Newton and linked through possession.

Armswell Farm began as a place fed by 'the stream of a woman called Eormengyth'. Beaulieu Wood does not have the usual meaning for such a place name, this is not from the Old French for 'beautiful view', and indeed we would expect this to have evolved to Beoley for this is from *beo leah*, 'the woodland clearing frequented by bees'. Bookham Farm is a corruption of 'Bubba's *cumb* or valley'; Brockhampton Farm describes 'the home farm by the brook'; Chaston Farm was the *tun* or farmstead of the family of Richard and William Chavel; and Clinger Farm describes 'the clayey wooded slope'.

Cosmore lies between two streams and has a name from a British word related to Welsh *cors* and Old English *mor*, both of which mean 'marshland'. Duntish sees Old English *dun* with a word that must be related to Goth *atisk*, 'cornfield', and Old High German *ezzisch*, 'piece of land', and thus describing the 'cultivated land on a slope'. Henley is a common name that always refers to 'the woodland clearing of hens (of wild birds)' from *henn leah*.

Monkwood Hill is a reminder that much of the manor of Buckland Newton belonged to Glastonbury Abbey; Plush is from Old English *plysc* meaning 'pool'; Revels Farm is named from the family of Richard Ryvel, here by 1325; Sharnhill Green tells us it was 'the hill with a cairn'; while the 'woodland clearing by the steep ridge or bank' is today known as Stickley Coppice.

Barnes's Lane was home to the family of Thomas Barnes by 1645; Harvey's Farm was associated with Widow Harvey in 1664; the family of Oliver Laurence were living at Laurence's Farm by 1688; Lockett's Lane was home to Giles Lockett in 1664; John Lovelace and Widow Lovelace are recorded as being in Lovelace Lane at different times during the seventeenth century; Edward Miller was at Miller's Farm in the early seventeenth century; and Watts Hill was home to both Robert Wattes and Thomas Wattes in 1664.

Landscombe Lane is one of those places that conjures-up a vivid image simply by defining it; however, the reader shall have to produce their own image for *leman cumb*, which describes 'the valley of the sweethearts or lovers'.

At Buckland Newton locals can enjoy a drink at the Gaggle of Geese, a strange name for a pub, which probably points to what could be found here before the pub served its first drink. The sign depicts two geese (is this enough to be a gaggle?) fleeing, but had they been flying this pub would have been the Skein of Geese.

BURLESTON

Listed as Bordelestone in 934, this name is of Old English origin in 'the farmstead of a man called Burdel', with the suffix from tun.

BURSTOCK

Domesday records the name as Burewinestoch, which shows a Saxon personal name followed by *stoc*. This Old English term is used to describe a 'special place'; however, before any ideas of rituals, hauntings or similar are coined, we should remember that what is special to one is utterly meaningless to another. Hence the Saxon *stoc* is usually referring to 'the outlying place', somewhere belonging to the main body of the settlement and used for grazing, agriculture, and possibly even a meeting place. Thus the name can be said to be 'the outlying farmstead of a woman called Burgwynn, or of a man called Burgwine'.

BURTON BRADSTOCK

A name recorded in Domesday as Bridetone in 1086. This, as examined under Long *bredy* and Littlebredy, comes from the Celtic river name *bredy* meaning 'the gushing or surging stream' and the Old English *tun* or 'farmstead', and thus the Bride forms the first element of Burton and not that of Bradstock as would be expected. The addition of Bradstock is from the Abbey of Bradenstoke who held this manor from at least the thirteenth century.

Chapter 3

Cale to Crichell

CALE (RIVER)

A river name of uncertain origins, Cale was found as Cawel and Wincawel in 956, which seem to refer to separate arms of the same River Cale. Whilst the present river name is unknown, the one tenth-century record certainly shows this to be preceded by a British word akin to Welsh *gwyn* meaning 'white'.

CANFORD (MAGNA & LITTLE)

A place name that means 'the ford of a man called Cana' can safely be assumed to have once been a single place with one (Little) an off-shoot of the other (Magna). The term *magna* is the Latin word for 'great' and — we must assume — Little Canford was one referred to with the Latin affix of *parva* meaning 'little'. However, records of this name show no Latin form at all, but show the etymology in English as Cheneford in 1086, Kaneford in 1195, Lytel Canefford in 1381, and Greate Canford in 1612.

The name of Ashington is derived from Old English *aesc haeme tun*, or 'the farmstead of the dwellers by the ash trees'; Lake Farm is derived from *lacu* or 'small stream', which is a tributary of the Stour; Merley Hall Farm tell us this place started as 'the woodland clearing by a pool'; while Oakley is a common name, always referring to 'the woodland clearing by the oak trees'.

Arrowsmith Road is named after the family of Edward Arrowsmith, who were here by 1799; Bishop's Cottages refer to the family of William Bysshopp, here by 1543; Pergin's Island refers to John Perham, here by 1463; the name of Tulgey Wood was undoubtedly taken from Lewis Carroll's Jabberwocky, although why is unknown; Waterloo Reservoir is taken from the Waterloo Iron Foundry; and Trunk Hole, a box with holes or perforations allowing fresh water to pass through, which was pegged in the River Stour to keep fish alive until they were taken for the table.

CANN

A strange sounding place name, Cann is typical of the topographical descriptions used by the Saxons, for they employed words that likened the shape to an object rather than naming the shape itself. This name is recorded as Canna in the twelfth century, coming from Old English *canne* and referring to 'a can or cup', and it tells of a region where the settlement lies in 'a hollow, or deep valley'.

Anketil's Place marks the site of that family's manor house, and the family have been mentioned in the county since the record of Roger Ancketil in Shaftesbury during the thirteenth century. Blynfield Farm takes its name from 'the *feld* or open land of the stream called Blinch', the river name from *blinc* meaning 'the glittering or sparkling stream'. While Guy's Marsh must be named after someone with this Old French name, it should be noted there is no record of any person with this name.

Records of Holm and Ivy Farm show the name comes from Old English *holegn* or dialect *holm* describing 'the holly thicket'. There is no etymological reason for the addition of Ivy and the addition seems to be due to the convential association of the two plants. Lydford Farm is from *glida ford*, or 'the ford frequented by a bird of prey (such as a kite)'. Bishop's Farm was home to Roger Bishop in 1316; Cole's Lane remembers William Cole, who was here in the early fifteenth century; Mathew and Christopher Grene were working Green's Farm by 1664; Mayor Farm was home to Thomas Mayo, also from at least 1664; Paynthouse Farm comes from Middle English pentis describing 'an outhouse or shed with a sloping roof'; and by 1427 Robert Wilkyns was working at what is now known as Wilkin's Farm.

CASTLETON

A name recorded as Casteltone in 1327 and as Casteltoun in 1452, this name comes from Old English and describes 'the farmstead by the castle'. The castle in question is Sherborne Castle, built in the twelfth century.

Bedmill Copse and Bedmill Farm are from *byden myln*, 'the mill fed from the hollow'; Blackmarsh really is 'the dark-coloured marshland'; Honeycomb Cottages and Honeycomb Wood mark the 'valley where honey is produced'; Overcombe was 'the upper valley'; Pinford markes 'the pine tree ford'; while the names of Silverlake Cottages and Silverlake Farm began life as *seofon lacu*, a corruption of the 'seven springs or streams'.

Clatcombe refers to itself as 'the valley where burdock grows'; there really was dancing at Dancing Hill; Half Moon Clump is named from its shape; Jerusalem is a name given to a hill in Sherborne Park; Redhole Lane describes itself as 'the reedy hollow'; and Sir Walter Raleigh's Seat is a reminder of a former owner of Sherborne Castle.

CATHERSTON LEWESTON

A name where the earliest surviving record comes from 1268 as Chartreston. The next record of this place name comes from 1316, when the name is quite different as Lesterton. Clearly the modern form is a combination of these two and is itself a big clue to the origin of this place. A glance at the history of this area around the end of the thirteenth century shows there were two settlements here at that time, where the names of the respective families are seen as Charteray-tun and Lester-tun. Adjacent for many decades, it was almost inevitable they would merge to form a single settlement. Yet we would normally expect to find one being eventually dominant and a single place name to survive.

CATTISTOCK

Domesday records this name as Stoche and by Cattestok in 1208. This name comes from Old English *stoc* and referring to 'the outlying place, the secondary settlement'. The late thirteenth century addition comes from the manorial addition of the Catt family who were here by the thirteenth century.

CAUNDLE (BISHOP'S & PURSE)

Two place names that have given toponymists (those with an interest in the origin of place names) much trouble. Records of this name are found as Candel in 1086, Purscaundel in 1241, and Caundel Bisops in 1294, with only one of these elements ever having been defined with any certainty. The meaning of Caundle has baffled for years for no equivalent has ever been traced. It has been said to be a name for the hills around here and yet it is unwise to speculate without further evidence. The additions are clearly to differentiate between the two. While Bishop's Caundle was certainly the possession of the Bishop of Salisbury, the name of Purse Caundel is presents a different problem and although it is almost certainly the name of a manorial family there is no documented evidence to support this theory.

Caundle Wake derives its name from Ralph Wake, who was lord of this manor in 1290; Blind Lane tells us it was 'leading nowhere'; Giles's Lane was associated with the family of William Gele in 1327; Laines Plantation comes from *leyne*, which describes 'a tract of arable land'; and Ryall's Farm and Ryall's Lane are from Old English *ryge hyll* and speak of 'the rye hill'.

Purse Caundle features minor names such as Russon, 'the valley where rushes grow', and a name also seen in erroneously recorded as Hussen Hanging, with *hangra* or 'steep slope'; In Caundle Brake the addition 'Brake' describes 'a thicket'; Clayhanger refers to 'a wood on a steep hillside'; Crendel comes from *crundel* or 'the quarry'; Hanover Hill has no connection with that part of Germany, this is from *heah ofer* or 'the high ridge'; Plumley Wood gets its name form 'the woodland clearing where plum trees grow'; Rue Lane is bordered by a 'row of trees'; and Trip's Farm is named after the family of Richard Tripp, here by 1332.

CAUNDLE MARSH

Among the many old records of this name include Kaundel Mareys in 1234, la Merse in 1244, and Merssh Kaundel in 1311. As with the previous name, the origins of Caundle are very uncertain, but the addition is undoubtedly Old English *mersc* meaning 'marsh', a name by which this place was known several times.

Local names include Ashcombe Farm, 'the valley where ash trees grow'; Prytown Farm, which refers to itself as 'the estate of the Pride family', and Nicholas and Richard Pride were here in 1327; Hawkins's Farm, which was worked by the family of Joan Hawkins in 1614 and Giles Hawkins fifty years later; Pleck Cottages, which are found at 'the small plot of land'; and Tut Hill, which stems from Old English *tot hyll* and describes 'the look-out hill'.

'The street of farmers', Cerne Abbas.

Poll Bridge Farm is an interesting name, and the modern name has only been seen since the sixteenth century and describes 'the bridge by the pool'. Prior to this there are records of this name as Deuelepole in 1280, Develpol in 1332, and Dellepol in 1428, a name that is derived from *deofel pol* and describes 'the devil pool'. Note that this does not refer to Satan but more generally to any devil or mischievous sprite, a surprisingly common reference in water names.

CERNE ABBAS

Nationally better known for the chalk figure here, it is often overlooked that there is a settlement of this name here. Domesday gives this as simply Cernel, yet by 1288 this is seen as Cerne Abbatis. The two elements have quite different origins: the addition is clearly a reference to this being held by the local abbey, while the main name comes from a Celtic river name. Here is the name of the River Cerne, itself taken from a Celtic term *carn* meaning 'cairn, heap of stones'. Now, even today, a cairn is a marker and it is easy to see this as the same thing historically, although whether this was a marker for this place or if it was a route marker is unclear.

Local names include Acerman Street, telling of the 'place of the farm workers', and Andrews Lane, which was home to the family of Samuel Andrews.

The local pub is the Cerne Giant, and the chalk figure has been the subject of much debate in recent times as to its age. Generally thought to be at least Saxon and even

The giant on the hill at Cerne Abbas.

The Giant Inn, Cerne Abbas.

pre-Roman, there is no mention of this figure before the seventeenth century. By cutting trenches 1-foot wide and 1-foot deep, a figure of a naked man has been created, standing 180-foot high and 157-foot wide. In 1996, archaeologists discovered his left hand had once held a cloak and there had been a disembodied head at his feet. No conclusion was reached as to the age of the figure, or of who or what it represents. Doubtless the arguments will continue for some time to come.

CERNE (NETHER & UP)

No surprise to find this has identical beginnings to the previous name, coming from the Celtic river name of the River Cerne. The additions here are first seen in 1206 as Nudernecerna and in 1086 as Obcerne, being taken from Old English *neotherra*, 'lower down', and Old English *upp*, 'higher up'.

Here Bazon Hill is derived from 'Baell or Baelli's hill'; Cank Farm and High Cank share a name from Old English *canc*, or 'steep and rounded hill'; Fernycombe Coppice lies at the 'valley where ferns grow'; Wancombe Bottom and Wancombe Hill are associated with 'the tumulus overlooking the valley'; Wether Hill is 'the hill where wethers or castrated rams are reared'; and Whistle Barn is recorded as White Barn in 1811, but the real origin is seen earlier as being at 'the west hill'.

CHALBURY

The earliest surviving record of this name comes from 946 as Cheoles burge. This is derived from a Saxon personal name and Old English *burh*, and describing 'the fortified place associated with a man called Ceol'.

Within this parish is found Didlington Farm, a well-documented name that refers to 'the farmstead associated with a man called Dydel', the personal name preceding Old English *ing tun*. Historically, this name is important, for the boundaries noted in a Saxon charter are identical to those of the modern Chalbury. Thus Didlington is not simply a minor name but was an alternative name for the parish. Duke's Copse is a reminder that this manor was held by the duchy of Lancaster by 1427.

CHALDON (EAST & HERRING)

The basic name here comes from Old English *cealf-dun* and meaning 'the hill where calves are grazed'. The additions here are to distinguish the two: East is self-explanatory and Herring is a rather corrupted form of Hareng, the family who were lords of this manor from at least the twelfth century. These names are listed as Celvedune in 1086 and Chaluedon Hareng in 1243.

West Fossil Farm is easy to link with the Jurassic Coast, but it has nothing to do with fossils from the etymological viewpoint. This is most likely from Old English *forst hyll* and describes 'the west hill with a ridge'. Tadnoll Mill is from *tadde halh* or *hol* giving 'the toad infested nook or hollow'. Bat's Head is indeed a promontory, but it does not resemble the small flying mammal, so it must either have been where these nocturnal creatures had a roost, or perhaps this is simply a personal name. Looking offshore we see two rocks known as the Cow and the Calf, and as they are of different sizes it is easy to see which is which. Gostelowes Farm reminds us that Richard Gostelowe built here in 1728. While the much-eroded promontory that is Swyre Head merits a name meaning 'the neck of land'.

It seems that wherever you are in Dorset there is some reminder of the coast being within easy reach. One landlord or owner was keen to remind others of his former life when he named this local pub the Sailors Return. Later, the sign painter depicted his wife welcoming the sailor home from his voyages; however, in the background her lover is hiding in a cupboard. Was this sign painted by a woman who had had enough of hearing sailors having a girl in every port and had decided to depict how a wife could be justified in having her own fun?

CHARLTON MARSHALL

Charlton is a very common place name which, coming from Old English *ceorl tun*, describes 'the farmstead of the freemen or peasants' and is the very reason as to why it is so common. Invariably there is an addition and here it is the name of the family who held this manor by the thirteenth century. This place is recorded as Cerletone in 1086 and as Cherleton Marescal in 1288. The local public house also takes the name, being called the Charlton Inn.

Birch Close was formerly known as Brunes Close, a name from the family of William le Brune who were here in 1301, although the reason for the change of name is uncertain. Gorcombe Cottages and Gorcombe Wood share an element, which is either from *gara cumb*, 'the point of land in the valley', or *GOR cumb*, 'the dirty or muddy valley'.

CHARMINSTER

Domesday shows this to be Cerminstre, clearly the 'church on the River Cerne', with the suffix from Old English *mynster*. The river name means 'cairn' and is explained under Cerne Abbas.

Local names here include Forston, meaning 'Forsard's manor' and remembering the home of William Forsard's family who were here by 1285; Herrison is derived from 'Hareng's *tun* or farmstead'; Pulston Barn comes from 'Pullein's farmstead'; Wolfeton House was built on what used to be 'Wulfa's farmstead'; Walls Coppice is adjacent to the site of a former Roman villa, hence the name; and Sodern (which was Soddern Bridge in 1791) is from an early Modern English sodom used to mean 'wicked place', although just why this was considered 'wicked' is unclear.

At Charminster a drink can be had at the Three Compasses, a device featured in several coats of arms but when specifically three pairs of compasses this can only be a reference to a carpenter, presumably a former landlord had trained in this trade. One can also enjoy a glass near the golf course, the pub aptly named the Caddy.

Forston village sign.

CHARMOUTH

A name recorded as Cernemude in 1086 is evidence that this place name meaning 'the mouth of the River Char', may not always have been so named. Indeed the place name seems to have influenced a river name that was once identical in meaning (if not also form) as the Cerne, discussed under Cerne *abbas* and referring to a 'cairn'. This would not have been a deliberate change but would have occurred naturally through local pronunciation.

CHEDINGTON

Found in 1194 as Chedinton, here is a name derived from a Saxon personal name and Old English *ing tun*, which tells us of 'the farmstead associated with a man called Cedd or Cedda'.

The local is the Winyards Gap Inn, which has taken a local place name of uncertain meaning and origin.

CHELBOROUGH

With Domesday's offering of Celberge the only early record to work with, there are three possible origins for this place name. If this is a Saxon name with Old English *beorg* then we are looking at 'the hill of a man called Ceola'. However, if the first element is

Old English *ceole* then this is 'the hill in the gorge' and literally the 'throat of the land, or this may represent Old English *elac* and speaking of the 'chalk hill'.

CHESELBOURNE

Listed in 869 as Chiselburne and as Ceseburne in 1086, this is a name which comes from Old English *cisel burna* and describing this as the '(place at) the gravel stream'.

Minor names here include Bramblecombe Lane, which runs along 'the valley where the brambles grow'; Lyscombe Bottom is from *lisc cumb* or 'the valley where reeds grow'; Yetman's Barn reminds us of the family of Thomas Yateman, here by 1664; while self-expanatory names include Round Copse, Nine Cornered Copse and Nineteen Acre Hanging an area on 'the steep slope'.

CHESIL BEACH

This name is not found earlier than 1540, as Chislle bank, yet the form tells us it must surely have existed centuries before this. This name comes from Old English *cisel* and means 'shingle', a most apt description of this 18-mile pebble reef, which is part of the famed Jurassic Coast. The bank of shingle is of varying sized pieces, and the further southeast the smaller the shingle. Smugglers claimed they could tell exactly where they had landed on Chesil Beach even in total darkness, simply be examining the size of the stones underfoot. It was from the shingles bank that the village of Chesil took its name, for that is not recorded until 1608.

CHETNOLE

Found in a document dated 1242 as Chetenoll, this name speaks of 'Ceatta's hillock' and features a Saxon personal name followed by Old English *cnoll*.

CHETTLE

If Domesday's record of *Ceotel* is considered accurate then this must be Old English ceotel and saying that this was the '(place in) the deep valley'.

Hatts Coppice describes 'the hat shaped hill'; Yonder Brawflings is a field name referring to 'the broad furlongs'; and Burts Close remembers William Burt, here in 1664.

CHICKERELL

A name recorded in Domesday as Cicherelle, this has never been adequately explained and no potential etymology can be suggested.

Local names include Putton, which historically would have been expected to become Puttington from a Saxon personal name and Old English *inga tun* and thus describing 'the farmstead associated with a man called Puda'. Crook Hill is from British *crug* and Old English *hyll*, thus meaning 'hill, hill'. Tidmoor Point comes from Old English *tide mor* and warning that this was 'the marshy ground reached by the flood tide'.

Local pubs include the Victoria, which commemorates the nation's longest-serving monarch, reigning for sixty-four years. While the name of the Turks Head Inn is often associated with the Saracen's Head, here it was probably a maritime reference to the Turks Head knot, used for both practical and decorative purposes on a boat.

CHIDEOCK

An unusual modern form for a place name, which can be explained because it features Celtic elements influenced by Saxon pronunciation and corruption. This name is found in Domesday as Cidihoc in 1086, it comes from Old English *ced* meaning 'wood'. It is not, as is often suggested, a name from the River Chid. Indeed this is a river name named from the process known as back-formation — that is, named after the place and not vice versa.

The Clock House Inn is the local pub, although today there is no outward sign of the clocks that gave it a name.

CHILCOMBE

This name means 'the valley at a hill-slope called Cilte', which is an early hill name that has not been explained or defined, and it is followed by Old English *cumb*. The place is recorded in Domesday as Ciltecombe in 1086.

CHILD OKEFORD

Listed as Acford in 1086 and as Childacford in 1227, this name comes from Old English *ac ford* or 'the oak tree ford'. The addition is from Old English *cild* and tells of the 'noble born son', a reference to some early owner.

Local names include Fontmell Parva, 'the smaller settlement on the river near the bare hill', where the Celtic river name is followed by Latin *parva*. Hambledon Hill refers to the archaeological remains of the Neolithic enclosure and Iron Age hill fort as 'the scarred, mutilated hill'.

Hayward Bridge does not come from Old English *heage weard* meaning 'hedge keeper', every record before the eighteenth century shows this was Heyford Bridge and thus describes 'the ford used at haymaking'. Two other names that have potentially confusing origins are Nicholas's Copse, which is often said to point to the church dedicated to St Nicholas, and yet there is a Mrs Nicholls recorded much closer to the place in 1664, and the name of Terrace Coppice, which is a surname, either Tarry or Terry depending upon which record is correct.

The local pub is the Saxon Inn. Not exactly dating from the Saxon era, these three cottages were constructed in the seventeenth century. It was an off-licence until 1950, when it became the New Inn and the pub was not known as the Saxon Inn until 1965.

Christchurch Priory.

CHILFROME

Listed in Domesday as simply Frome, the addition is first seen in a document dated 1206 as Childefrome. Here Old English *cild* is added to the river name to speak of 'the estate on the River Frome of the young men'. This is a Celtic or British river name meaning 'bright, brisk'.

CHRISTCHURCH

A name which was recorded as Twynham prior to the arrival of the Normans, a name meaning 'the place between the rivers' and derived from Old English *betweonan ea*. However, by 1125 this name is seen as Christecerce, which comes from Old English *Crist cirice* and, somewhat predictably, means 'the Church of Christ'.

Local place names here include Druitt Road and Druitt House, which now serves as the library, and was built by James Druitt (1816-1904) in 1844. Druitt served five terms as mayor, was also a Justice of the Peace, held the office of Town Clerk, and while away from his life as a public servant also managed to find time to pursue careers as a solicitor and to speculate in the property market. He also had an unusual connection with the murders in 1888 attributed to the infamous Jack the Ripper. James had a brother, William Druitt, whose son Montague was recovered from the River Thames

The road to Christchurch.

at Chiswick complete with suicide note. He is one of the three prime suspects in the seemingly timeless investigations.

Drapper Road is named after John Draper, whose family were clearly drapers but who personally was the last prior of Christchurch serving 1520-39. Galton Avenue was named after Douglas Galton, who held the office of mayor during the Second World War. Another mayor, Thomas Beckley, who served during the nineteenth century, came from a family of landowners who are commemorated by the name of Beckley Copse. The twentieth century history of Christchurch cannot fail to mention its links with air travel. Thankfully, the planners recognised this link when naming streets and thus we have The Runway, De Havilland Way, Dakota Close, Catalina Close, Comet Way, Donnington Drive, Pipers Drive, Halifax Way, Airspeed Road, Sunderland Drive, Wellesley Avenue, and Viscount Drive.

Local pubs include the Sandpiper, a wading bird, which would find the perfect habitat around the coastline and mudflats of Christchurch.

CHURCH KNOWLE

Domesday's record of Cnolle shows the Old English element *cnoll* meaning 'hill top'. Later the name is recorded as Churchecnolle in 1346, where the addition is clearly from Old English *cirice* meaning 'church'.

Minor names include Barnston Farm, from 'Beorn's farmstead'; Bradle Farm is 'the broad woodland clearing'; Bucknowle refers to 'Bubba's hill top'; East Creech is from a British word allied to Proto-Welsh *crug* and describing 'the eastern barrow or hill'; Whiteway Farm lies near what would have been a consipicuously chalky road across the hill; Madgrove is not questioning anyone's sanity but is derived from *maed grafa*, or 'the woodland grove by a meadow'; and Newfoundland cannot have been newly discovered and therefore must be a cryptic reference to a far flung corner of the parish, as would have seemed the Canadian island at the time.

CLIFTON MAYBANK

There are records of Clifton Maybank as Cliftun in 1002, Clistone in 1086, and as Clifton Mabank in 1319. Here the Old English *cliffe tun* tells us of 'the farmstead by the cliff or bank' and which was the manor of one William Malbeenc in 1084, Maybank is an Old French name found several times in England, in almost as many different forms.

COLEHILL

A common name, from Old English *coll-hyll* meaning 'hill hill' or *col-hill*, 'the hill where charcoal is produced'.

Local names include Leigh, from Old English *leah* and normally seen with a second element. However, here it stands alone and simply describes 'the woodland clearing'. The corruption of *wuduc* worth to Wilksworth Farm seems unlikely, thus there must have been another (unknown) place name which influenced such a development. This Old English name refers to 'the enclosure of the small wood'.

Other names found here are Burt's Hill, referring to the family of William Burt who were here by 1664; Deans Grove, named after the Dean of Wimborne who had holdings here; Dogdean Lane and Dogdean Farm, probably stemming from *docce denu*, 'the valley of the dock plant', rather than *dogga denu*, 'the valley of dogs'; Elliott's Grave comes from Old English *graef* meaning 'pit' and was associated with Thomas Elliott who was here in 1664; Little Lonnen is a slurred version of a tongue-in-cheek name for a very small hamlet that began as 'Little London'; Merry Field Hill marks the place where 'merriment and games took place'; and Catley Copse was 'the woodland glade frequented by wild cats', which does not refer to the Scottish wild cat, a highly territorial and solitary creature, but to feral cats.

The local is the Horns Inn, a pub name that most often refers to the horn sounded by the drayman to announce his imminent arrival.

COMPTON ABBAS

Listings of this name begin with Cumtune in 956, as Cuntone in 1086, and as Cumpton Abbatise in 1293. From the 'farmstead in a valley' and Old English *cumb tun*, this name later has an addition referring to it being 'of the abbess' from Latin *abbatisse* and a reference to its early possession by Shaftesbury Abbey.

Hawkcombe Lane takes the name of several fields around here, these derived from Old English *hol cumb* describing 'the hollow or deep valley'. Twyford Farm is a name found across England, always referring to the 'double ford' and often unclear whether this refers to two parallel fords or a ford crossing two streams, but here it is obvious the latter is the case. Baker's Farm was once home to Thomas Baker; Glyn Farm was associated with Sir Richard Carr Glyn who bought the manor in 1809; Tucker's Farm is associated with the family of John Tucker, who were here by 1564; and Prystock Farm is from *preost stoc*, or 'the outlying place of the priests'.

COMPTON (NETHER & OVER)

A record of Cumbtun in 998, as Contone in 1086, as Nethercumpton in 1288, and as Ouerecumton in 1268, with the basic place name coming from Old English *cumb-tun*, or 'the farmstead in the valley', and later suffixed by Old English *neotherra* and *iferra* meaning 'lower' and 'higher' respectively.

At Nether Compton we find minor names such as Stallen Farm referring to 'the stream with a stone channel'. There are two possible reasons for this culvert for this arm of the Trent Brook: either this was diverted to provide a supply of fresh water to a particular location or, as it is tempting to suggest, it was to prevent it from living up to its name meaning 'the wanderer' i.e. liable to flood.

The City is an ironic name for a very small settlement; Hart's Lane recalls former resident Nicholas Harte, here in 1563; the Round House was formerly a cold bathing house, renowned for the quality of its water in the middle of the nineteenth century; Smelland's Lane is derived from *smael land* or 'narrow strips of land'; Tucker's Cross was home to the family of Edward le Touker in 1340; and Guineagore Lane is named from *gara*, 'the triangular piece of land', with guinea possibly a tax or rent, but more likely a purchase price — a guinea being one pound one shilling, an amount still used when buying and selling horses.

At Over Compton, Chapel Plantation, not mentioned before the middle of the nineteenth century, likely occupies the site of the chapel recorded in documents dated 1291 and 1401. Marl Lane is the sole reminder of the marl pits once dug here.

COMPTON VALENCE

Another name that comes from 'the farmstead in the valley' and Old English *cumb-tun*, Compton Valence is first seen in Domesday as Contone. Later, this is found as Compton Valance, with the manorial addition referring to William de Calenca, Earl of Pembroke, who was here in the thirteenth century.

COMPTON (WEST)

Listings of this name record this place as Comptone in 934 and Contone in 1086. Later we find documented evidence of this being known as Compton Abbas, with identical origins to that place. However, to have two such places in the same county must have been very confusing and this place became 'the western farmstead in the valley'.

Corfe Castle.

COOMBE KEYNES

A name first seen in Domesday as simply Cume, the addition first appears in 1299 as Kaynes although within a century there are over a dozen different spellings of this personal name. This describes the '(place at) the valley' held by Willial de Cahaignes by 1199, and the family held this manor until at least the fourteenth century.

Other names here include Coombe Wood, or 'the woodland valley', although some records show this as Iveley, which would speak of 'the woodland clearing overgrown with ivy'. Kick Hill Coppice describes 'the look out hill', from a word related to Middle English *kiken* meaning 'to watch or peep'. Kimbert's End describes 'Cyma's pit'; Oakley Wood comes from 'the oak tree glade'; Rodford Withy Road leads to 'the reedy ford'; Row Down Coppice takes its name from 'the rough hill'; Clare Towers, gateway to Lulworth Park, is named after former resident Clare Weld who died in 1691; and Vary Coppice and Vary Clump share an origin in Old English *fearr* or *fearh*, referring to 'the bull or pig enclosure'.

CORFE CASTLE

Corfe Castle is found as *corf* in 955 and as Corffe Castell in 1302. The basic name comes from Old English *corf* meaning 'the cutting, gap, or pass'. Here the addition refers to the Norman castle, which was here by the twelfth century.

The village below Corfe Castle.

Locally we find the names of Afflington, referring to 'the farmstead of a woman called Aelfrun'; Ailwood or '(place at) the wood of a woman called Aethelgifu'; Brenscombe Farm began life as 'the valley of a man called Btyni'; Burberry Lane led to or past 'the hill with a cottage'; Challow Farm was worked by 'the cold spring or stream'; Encombe was known as 'the valley of the hens' — that is, hen birds in general and not simply chickens; Linch Farm was found at 'the ridge or bank'; Norden Farm refers to its position near 'the north hill'; Rempstone was 'the farmstead where wild garlic grows'; Rollington Farm began as 'the farmstead of a man called Raedl or Raedla'; Swyre tells us it was 'the neck of land'; and Woolgarston is derived from 'the farmstead of a man called Wulfgar'.

Countess Point is named for the Countess of Richmond; however, while Corfe Castle was repaired specifically for her to take up residence, the countess never lived here. Cuckoo Pound and Cuckolds Parlour probably both refer to cuckolding, thus these places should be understood as rendezvous points for lovers. Keeper's Copse likely refers to the home of one who was employed in the keep.

St Edward's Bridge reminds us that King Edward the Martyr was murdered at Corfe in 978 AD and it is for this reason the church is dedicated to him. There is also a St Edward's Fountain, a spring said to have healing powers.

For a monarch who is so venerated, historians see King Edward the Martyr's reign as ineffectual and very short; Edward reigned for less than three years from 8 July 975 to 18 March 978. His reign started in the worst possible way, accompanied by a comet visible to the naked eye, a dreaded harbinger of doom. Almost immediately, the land

Corfe footpath fingerpost.

was stricken by famine, while arguments with other nobles kept the land on the point of civil war. The circumstances behind his murder are confused with several different stories, each pointing elsewhere as the culprit.

It was not until after the king's body had lain at Wantage for over a year that his name was revered. When his body was to be removed and taken to Shaftesbury it was found to be as if he had been killed the day before and showed no signs of the normal deterioration after death. Immediately, a cult was born and his remains were given a lavish re-burial in Shaftesbury, with his relics placed in a more prominent position at the nunnery.

CORFE MULLEN

Another name meaning 'the cutting, gap, or pass', Corfe Mullen stems from Old English *corf*. This is exactly how it is seen in Domesday, as Corf, while the record of 1176 sees this as *corf* le Mullin. The addition here is from the Old French *molin* and telling us of 'the mill' here.

Local names here include Sleight, from Old English *slaeget* meaning 'the sheep pasture'; Upton is a common name meaning 'the higher farmstead', unusually there is no second element to distinguish this from other like-named places; Brog Street speaks of 'the place straggling the road by a stream'; Cherett's Clump is named after Thomas Cherett whose family were here by 1664; Lockyer's School owes thanks to the generosity of Richard Lockyer, here in 1730; and Naked Cross stood at a crossroads and was simply 'unadorned, plain', possibly even saying there were no directions on the marker should this name be of more recent origins.

The local pubs include the Dorset Soldier, a reference to one of the directors of the brewery who owned this pub having commanded the local regiment too.

CORSCOMBE

Documents show this was Corigescumb in 1014 and as Coriescumbe in 1086, a name coming from Old English *corf weg* and speaking of 'the valley of the road in the pass'. However, it may also be possible that the first element is an old name for a stream here, although if this is so the meaning is unknown.

The local Talbot Arms refers to the breed of dog, a white animal with black spots that was bred specifically for hunting and tracking.

CRANBORNE

A name restricted to Creneburne in 1086, which is from Old English *cran burna* and speaking of 'the stream frequented by cranes or herons'. The river name here, that of the Crane, is named from the place in a process known as back-formation.

Here too is Cranborne Chase, a name taken from the settlement and which features the additional Middle English element *chace* meaning 'tract of land for breeding and hunting wild animals' — literally a managed hunting area.

Castle Street is named from the nearby earthworks, which also gave a name to Castle Hill. Bellows Cross probably gets its name from Belly Lane, in turn leading to 'the bell-shaped hill'. Biddlesgate Farm is found in 1236 as Butelesheite, a name that tells us of 'Buttel's gate'. The names of Blagdon Farm, Blagdon Hill, and Blagdon Hill Wood share a common origin from *blaec dun* and describing 'the dark coloured hill'.

The origin of Boveridge depends upon whether the hill took the name of the place, in which case it comes from *bufan hrycg* and the '(place) above the ridge', or, if the hill was named first, it refers to 'the bow shaped ridge' from *boga hrycg*. Crockerton Hill is seen on a map of 1325 as Crokkerneweye, which appears to be from Old English *crocc aern weg* and describes the 'way to the hill of the potters'. Knap Barrow is 'the high tumulus' and not seen here but refers to the burial mound on the nearby county boundary.

Cranbourne Farm refers to 'the stream frequented by crane or heron'; Dead Man is the name of a crossroads, doubtless one where a corpse was found; Goddard's Barn recalls the family who were at Cranborne by the seventeenth century; Jack's Hedge Corner is from the family of Thomas Jackes, who were here by 1332; Pye Lane is either from *pie* meaning 'magpie' or *peo* referring to 'insects'; Salisbury Hall is a reminder that the earls of Salisbury have held this manor since the seventeenth century; and Standridge is from *stan hrycg* and refers to 'the stone ridge' and a line of stones that once marked the parish boundary.

Locals meet for a drink in the Sheaf of Arrows, a term describing a quiver full of arrows. Here the name is heraldic, a reference to the Cecil family who were living at Cranborne Manor.

CREECH (EAST)

A name coming from Celtic *crug*, 'a round hill', and referring originally to Creech Barrow here, the name is recorded as Criz in Domesday.

CRICHEL (LONG & MOOR)

Here the basic name comes from Celtic *crug* and Old English *hyll*, together meaning 'hill hill'. The distinctive additions here come from Old English *lang* and *mor* referring to 'long' and 'marshy ground' respectively.

Moor Crichel, sometimes given as More Crichel, features several minor place names of note. That of Chetterwood features three elements, Proto Welsh or Proto Cornish *ced* describing 'a woodland', either Proto Welsh or Proto Cornish *rid* meaning 'a ford', or Old English *rid* referring to the 'stream', with a more modern and self-explanatory 'wood'. Cockrow Farm tells us of 'the row of trees where woodcock are found', the bird being a much prized delicacy; Manswood is a corruption of mange referring to the skin disease of animals produced by a parasite, and here the wood was thought to harbour such a parasite; Petty's Coppice was associated with Edward Petty in 1664; and Six Cross Ways really does mark the point where half a dozen lanes converge.

Long Crichel has minor names such as Bayton's Coppice, from the family of Bainton who held the manor of Crichel Lucy between 1411 and 1543. While Coutman's Croft is a corruption of Cookeman, of which there have been several generations in this parish since the seventeenth century. Prince's Coppice remembers the family of Thomas Prynce, who were here by 1547. While Veiny Cheese Pond is named from its resemblance to blue vinny cheese; 'vinny' is Dorset dialect for 'mouldy'.

Chapter 4

Dewlish to Durweston

DEWLISH

Here is a name recorded as Devenis in 1086 and as Deueliz in 1194, and it comes from an original Celtic river name describing 'the dark stream'.

Chebbard Farm takes the element *bord* and seems to be describing 'the board or plank of or near the boundary'. The local pub is the Oak at Dewlish; a large and striking tree was as obvious as any pub sign in times past, and indeed the pub sign began as a tree stripped of its lower branches to which a sheaf of barley was tied. Known as an ale stake, this was the forerunner of the modern pub sign and explains why so many trees are seen in pub names.

DORCHESTER

Dorchester is a name with a long recorded history, starting with Durnovaria in the fourth century, Dornwaraceaster in 814, and Dorcestre in Domesday. While the first element is not recorded, it can be seen as being related to other Celtic languages (such as Welsh, Irish, Breton, and Cornish) and precedes Old English *ceaster* as 'the Roman place of the fist-sized pebbles'. Furthermore, we can be fairly certain this fourth-century record represents the Celtic name for the town.

Street names here tell their own history. Barne's Way recalls former resident Robert Barnes, here in 1574; Damer's Road was home to Benjamin Dam'er in 1664; Durngate led to 'the hidden gate'; and Great Western Road provided access to the old GWR station.

Local names include Fordington, clearly 'the farmstead at the fording place'; Colliton House describes 'Coll's houses' and is a pet form of Colin or perhaps Nicholas; Friary Saw Mill belonged to the Franciscan Friary, the mills being built in 1485; Loud's Mill was worked by Thomas de Lude in 1304; Top 'o' Town is of obvious meaning, it refers to the higher, western end of High West Street; and Pindbury comes from 'Puna's fortification'. Maumbury marks the site of a pre-English earthwork, a Neolithic henge monument, which were later used by the Romans as an amphitheatre and was named by the Saxons as *malm burh*, or 'the fortification of sandy or chalky soil'.

Public houses here include the Junction, built when the railway came to the county town. The Original Thomas Hardy tells its own story for, while it clearly pays tribute to Dorset's most famous wordsmith, the addition tells us there was once an argument regarding duplication of the pub name. Another writer is commemorated by the late Poet Laureate, Ted Hughes (1930-98), whose personal life made the headlines almost as much as his published works.

The Chalk & Cheese is a perfect pub name, if somewhat unusual, for it has two elements linked by '&', and both words have identical phonetic initials (aliteration is an advertiser's dream). The name describes the area of chalkland and mentions the Blue Vinney cheese, which is synonymous with Dorset. The oddly named Blue Raddle refers to a door or gate made by weaving wooden laths between stronger upright poles, or raddles, and the colour can only be pertinent to this place.

The sign of the Wise Man hangs outside three seventeenth-century cottages, which were converted to the pub in 1937. On the sign is depicted an honest lawyer who recites the following:

I trust no wise man will condemn
A cup of genuine now and then
When you are faint, your spirits low
Your string relaxed: 'twill bend your bow

An odd verse, which is said to have been penned by Thomas Hardy, yet this seems unlikely as he would have had to have written this at least nine years before the pub served its first drink (Hardy died in 1928). Further conclusive proof is found in the lines, for Thomas Hardy had talent.

DORSET

The name of the county has no record known before that of Dornsaetum in the ninth century. This name tells us it was referred to as 'the territory of the people of Dorn', the place name being a reduced form of Dornwaraceaster and referring to Dorchester (see above) with the Old English suffix *saete*.

DRIMPTON

A typical Old English place name, with a Saxon personal name and the common element *tun* and telling us it was 'Dreama's farmstead'. The name is not found before 1244 as Dremeton.

DUNTISH

A name recorded in 1249 as Dunhethis and which comes from the Old English *dun-etisc* and tells us this was 'the pasture on a hill'.

DURDLE DOOR

An unusual name indeed, and a name wihotut an obvious origin, for there is not a single record surviving before 1811 as Dirdale Door. However, the name must have been in use since shortly after the Norman Conquest, maybe even prior to that landmark historical event, for the name fits an Old English origin quite perfectly. It is thought to be from *thyrelod* meaning 'pierced' and *duru* meaning 'door or opening'. It is understood as meaning a place where an entry point was created through a natural barrier, probably vegetation but possibly a bank of earth, to reach whatever lay beyond — maybe a natural clearing and desirable pasture.

If this definition is accurate, then it would have afforded a natural enclosure for livestock and trapped them within, courtesy of the 'door', thus meaning the herdsman could be doing other work and not have to watch over his charges every single minute, as was the case with the Saxon *feld*. While this may appear to be the same as the modern field, it referred to the space within rather than a permanent and unbroken barrier around, as we would expect today. Indeed there were no fences or hedgerows surrounding a *feld*. Another clue to the use of this place comes from the use of *duru* 'door' rather than *geat* 'access point', the difference in that the latter (while obviously the forerunner of 'gate') refers to the road or path leading to (and from) the *feld*, not to any five-bar feature which we would expect today. It may be that this place was one of the earliest closed and locked fields or paddocks to have existed, indeed that the name even exists suggests it was something quite different for all names refer specifically to one place or person, it identifies.

DURWESTON

Not found before 1086 in Domesday as Derwinestone, this easily seen as 'Deorwine's *tun* or farmstead'.

Local names include Knight Farm, a common name that refers to 'the farm of the thanes or those in the employ of important persons'. Enford bottom is from Old English *ened ford* or 'the duck ford' across the River Stour. Pressham Wood comes from Old English *preost hamm* or 'the hemmed in land of the priests', that is belong to the church. While the name of the Rectory is self-explanatory, the interesting record is from 1784 as Parsonage Pexy'shole, with the extra reference to 'the hollow haunted by a pixie or pixies'.

Chapter 5

East Stoke to Eype

EAST STOKE

A name recorded as Stoches in 1086, Stokes in 1166, and Stok in 1284, this name is one of the most common in the land. Here it comes from Old English *stoc* and refers to 'the secondary or outlying settlement'. The addition refers to it being east of other places containing this element.

Local names include Binnegar, from Old English *bean hangra* or 'the slope where beans are grown'. Hethfelton is derived from Old English *haeth feld tun*, the farmstead of the heath-covered open land'. Luckford Coppice stands alongside 'Lugga's ford', the name later being seen as a family name of Robert Lug and William Lugg in the early fourteenth century. Rushton was 'the farmstead where rushes grow'; Stokeford describes 'the ford near to Stoke'; Baker's Well was home to Thomas Baker of Arne in 1650; Lytchet Bridge crosses the 'stream of the bog'; and Bunker's Hill is probably an allusion to the battle of that name in America in 1775.

EDMONDSHAM

Found in Domesday as Amedesham, this name may seem quite obvious and has changed little from Saxon times. However, while this is true, the lack of any early comparative forms to the rather unreliable proper names found in Domesday, makes defining either element here uncertain. It is clear that the suffix here is either *ham* 'homestead' or *hamm*, which is used to describe several natural features but all are basically a place which is surrounded on two or three sides by natural barriers — perhaps a loop of a meandering stream, hills or vegetation. Similarly, the first element, while clearly a Saxon personal name, could be Eadmod, Eadmund or the like and can be likened to attempting to discern the difference between Michael, Mitchell, Michaela and Michelle (along with the numerous pet forms) from a single record a thousand years old written by a Frenchman in Latin and which describes Domesday perfectly.

Local names include Romford Bridge and Romford Mill, names that share a common origin in hrung ford, which tells us it was 'the ford marked by a pole'. Westworth Farm gets its name from 'the western enclosure'; Cock Row is near the 'place where woodcock are netted'; Gotham refers to 'the hemmed in land where goats are kept', the name being shared by Gotham Common, Gotham Copse and Gotham Farm; and the names of Pistle Down and Pistle Hill is a corruption of the word 'epistle' and a reference to passages from the scriptures being read during the annual ceremony of beating the bounds.

EVERSHOT

Records of this name include Tevesict in 1202 and Evershet in 1286, both of which come form Old English *eofor sceat* and describe 'the corner of land frequented by wild boars'. The difference in the two thirteenth century records is because the earlier one has been confused when spoken of as being *ate* or 'at' Evershot.

EYPE

This is a name from Old English *geap* meaning 'the steep place' and is recorded as Yepe in 1365.

Chapter 6

Farnham to Frome Vauchurch

FARNHAM

This place name is recorded in Domesday as Fernham, a name that is clearly from Old English fearn ham and describing this as 'the homestead where ferns grow'.

Half Hide Coppice and Half Hide Down are two names that refer to a manor of 'half a hide', which is how this manor is described in Domesday. Tollard Farnham is minor name, which adds the name of the family of Brian de Toullard, lords of the manor in the thirteenth century and coming from Tollard Royal in Wiltshire, which lies across the border from Farnham. Downend Coppice comes from *dun ende* and describes 'the estate in the valley'.

FERNDOWN

Knowing the origin of the previous name, this may seem quite obvious; however, of the two potential origins neither have anything to do with ferns. The one early form is from 1321 as Fyrne, a name that could be Old English *fergen*, 'wooded hill', or *fierne*, 'fiery place', with the addition of Old English *dun* and used as 'down hill'.

Pubs here include the Night Jar, and the image of the bird also suggests a drink in the evening. The Pure Drop is another invitation: 'drop' can be interpreted as a small amount — except when used in the connection with pubs as in 'a drop too much to drink' when it can be any amount — but here the 'drop' is said to be of excellent quality. Found on the coat of arms of the Cutlers' Company, the elephant with a howdah on its back is interpreted as the Elephant & Castle. The Tap & Railway is in Station Road, pubs were often built to welcome thirsty travellers from the newly arrived railway, and the 'Tap' is always representative of the tapping of a barrel.

FIDDLEFORD

Here is a Saxon personal name and the Old English *ford*, which, recorded as Fitelford in 1224, speaks of 'Fitela's ford'.

FIFEHEAD (MAGDALEN & NEVILLE)

What might seem an unusual place name is actually quite easy to define. This is from Old English *fif-hid*, referring to 'five hides of land'. A hide is a measurement, not exactly of area but of productivity for it describes the amount of land required to feed one family for a single year. While this is usually given as equal to 30 acres, this is simply an average, for clearly more depends upon the quality of the land, what is being grown, and the size of the family than any amount of land. Here two similarly named places required additions for ease of recognition, Magdalen refers to the dedication of its church, while the de Nevill family held the other from at least the thirteenth century.

The parish of Fifehead Neville contains Lower Fifehead, which is sometimes referred to as Fifehead St Quintin, a place that was connected with Richard and Herbert de Sancto Quintino in 1205. These Normans could have originated from any of several places found in France called St Quentin. Brakethorne Copse is from Old English broc horn or 'the horn of land formed or bordered by a brook'. Cockrow Copse tells us this was 'the woodland clearing where woodcock were netted'; Dreadmoor Copse has earlier records as Deadmoor, in which case this is 'the disused moorland'; Smetherd Farm comes from *smiththe geard* and describes 'the yard with a smithy'; and Zoar Lane and Zoar Farm is probably a name referring to this region 'soaring' to some 300 feet.

At Fifehead Magdalen we find Trill Bridge, a name which is also seen in Trill Field and Trill Meadow and which reminds us of the family represented by Robert de Trul in 1268, Walter de Tril in 1316, and Walter Trul in 1327. While the bridge itself is across the River Stour, the name probably comes from a small stream that joins the Stour just below Trill Bridge. This name comes from Old English *tyrl*, which, as a stream name, describes it as 'that which turns or rolls along', clearly a lively or even turbulent stream.

Coking Lane leads to Coking Farm, together these show an origin of croccere and referring to the '(place of) the potters'. Earlier there were the names of Crokerford and Crokermill, although these names are now lost. Froghole Withy Bed refers to 'the hollow infested by frogs where willow grows'.

FLEET

We hardly need to refer to early records, such as that of Flete in 1086, to know this comes from Old English *fleot*. This refers here to a 'tidal creek'.

FOLKE

Listed as Folk in 1244, the name comes from the Old English *folc* and really does refer to this as being the '(land held by) the people'.

Local names include Allweston Farm describing 'Aelfheah or Aelfwig's farmstead'; Bishop's Down Farm shows that some of the land here was part of the possessions of the Bishop of Salisbury; Font Le Roi was until recently known as Fauntleroy Marsh, the name coming from the family of William Fauntleroi, here by the thirteenth century; Pin Bridge takes its name from pinc 'the bridge where minnows are seen'; Wizard Bridge and Wizard Lane are not what they seem but are a corruption of wise ford, 'the river or swamp ford'; Chaffey's Farm was worked by the family of Thomas Chafe by 1664;

Munden's Lane is a reminder of the family of John Munden, here in 1677; while Stakes Ford was 'the ford marked by stakes or posts' and the name was later transferred to Stakes Lane.

FONTMELL MAGNA

Found as Funtemel in 877, Fontemale in 1086, and as Magnam Funtemell in 1391, this is based on a Celtic river name speaking of it being 'the stream of or near the bare hill'. The addition is from Latin *magna* meaning 'great', which points to there being a *parva* or 'little' place so-named nearby.

Bedchester Farm describes 'Bedi's hyrst or wooded hill', the change to -chester from what should have become Bedhurst seems to have occurred during the sixteenth century although there is no rational explanation for this seemingly unique corruption. Blackven Farm describes 'the dark-coloured marsh'; Longcombe Bottom describes 'the long valley'; and Blatchford's Farm could have been transferred through a surname, although the description of 'the black or dark soil of the ford' would fit topographically.

Sixpenny Farm is not a reference to the rent, as we would normally expect from 'penny' names. Here the three elements are Old English *seaxe* and British *penn* thus describing 'the hill of the Saxons'. Woodbridge comes from *wudu brycg*, which is understood as 'the wooden bridge' rather than 'the wood by the bridge'. Gupple's Copse is an unusual name, which could be said to derive from the name of Maurice Gopyl who was here by 1327 or perhaps William Gopyld in 1332. However, there is no traceable or recognisable etymology for this surname, hence this may simply be a corruption of Goggs, a surname seen in Goggs Meadow.

FORATON

A document of 1236 gives this name as Forsadeston, featuring a family name and Middle English *toun*. Hence this is 'the estate of the Forsard family', who were known to have been here since the early thirteenth century and possibly earlier.

FRAMPTON

This name features a Celtic river name meaning 'the fair one' and seen today as one of the number of rivers said to be the Frome. Found in 1086 as Frantone this is 'the *tun* or farmstead on the River Frome'.

FROME ST QUINTIN

Frome St Quintin is another name that refers to the River Frome, a common Celtic stream name meaning 'the fair, fine, or brisk one' and here suffixed by the name of the St Quentin family who were here in the thirteenth century. Records of this name include

Litelfrome in 1086 and Fromequintin in 1288, and the earlier name can be seen as referring to this as 'the smaller settlement called Frome'.

FROME VAUCHURCH

Another settlement on the River Frome, this river name meaning 'the fair, fine, or brisk one'. Here a record of Frome Vaghechurche in 1297 shows the addition to refer to 'the coloured church'.

Chapter 7

Gillingham to Gussage

GILLINGHAM

Domesday records this name as Gelingeham, a name that comes from a Saxon personal name and Old English *inga ham* and tells us this was once 'the homestead of the family or followers of a man called Gylla'.

Local names include Hardings Lane, a reminder of the 'land of John Hardyng', who was here by 1313, and Hardings Hill. Bowridge is 'the bag-shaped ridge'; Eccliffe refers to the '(place at) Ecga's bank'; Forest Farm is the site of the former royal hunting forest; Huntingford was that 'ford used by the hunters'; Langham is a common name referring to 'the long hemmed in land'; Gutch Pool is difficult but probably comes from *gote* 'water course' or perhaps *gyte* meaning 'to pour forth'; and Bugley is either 'Bucge's woodland clearing' or the more intriguing *bugge* gives 'the woodland clearing of the boggary or hobgoblin'.

Bay is a place name from Early Modern English *bay* used to describe 'an embankment created to form a dam', it has also been transferred to Bay Bridge and Bay Farm. Clearly the present use of 'bay' describes a coastal inlet, rather different to the use here but one that does describe a similar feature but from the opposite viewpoint: i.e., today 'bay' refers to the water, while earlier 'bay' referred to the land rising above the water.

Madjeston features an Old German personal name and refers to this as 'Madalgar's manor'; Milton on Stour marks 'the middle farmstead on the River Stour'; Newbury House was 'the new manor house'; Pierston Farm was once an individual settlement, its name coming from 'Poer's manor'; Stock Farm began life as 'the secondary or outlying settlement'; Bainly Bottom was 'the woodland clearing where beans are grown'; while Bleet Lane seems to refer to this place being 'cold or bleak', for the adjective *bleat* meant 'wretched, miserable'.

Culvers Lane led to 'the dove cote'; Lanch Lane is a slurred land scearu and describes 'the boundary lane'; Lawn Bridge and Lawn Farm come from *launde* 'a forest glade'; Malthouse Farm has not seen a malthouse since the seventeenth century; Peacemarsh could well have seen some arguments, for the name describes 'the marshy land where peas are grown'; Waterloo Farm would have been given to this place to commemorate that landmark battle; and Slaughter Gate historically was known as 'Slander's gate', a surname which was influenced by the popular idea that this was was the site of the Battle of Penselwood in 1016, when many Danes were slaughtered.

Wyndlam Farm is located at 'the river meadow with a windlass', used for winching cargo to and from the river itself. Sandley is 'the sandy woodland clearing', although it has also been recorded with the alternative name of Sandhill and once, in 1902, as Stanley - which can only be an error and shows how easily mistakes can be made even in modern times.

The pubs of Gillingham include the Buffalo, a clear indication that this was a meeting place for the Royal Antediluvian Order of Buffaloes, a friendly society reformed in 1822. Note this refers to the African and Asian buffalo, not the North American bison, which is always known, erroneously, as the buffalo in the US. The Phoenix is named after the mythical bird that is consumed by fire every 500 years only to be reborn from the ashes. This name is often chosen for a pub that has undergone a major rebuild or re-opening. However, for the same reason it was chosen as a part of the Seymour family, dukes of nearby Somerset.

GLANVILLES WOOTTON

The basic name here comes from Old English *wudu tun* and is 'the farmstead of or in a woodland clearing'. The addition reminds us that the Glanville family were here from at least the thirteenth century, with the evolution of the name seen by the records of Widetone in 1086 and as Wotton Glauunnuill in 1288.

GOATHILL

Found as Gatelme in 1086 and Gathulla in 1176, this place comes from Old English *gat hyll* and is 'the hill where goats are pastured'.

GODMANSTONE

Here is a Saxon personal name suffixed by Old English *tun* and describing 'the farmstead of a man called Godmann', with the name seen as Godemanestone in 1166.

GOREWOOD

A name found throughout England and nearly always from Old English *gara wudu* or 'the triangular woodland'.

GUSSAGE (ALL SAINTS & ST MICHAEL)

No surprise to find these two nearby settlements are clearly distinguished by the additions, themselves easily seen as referring to the dedication of their respective churches. What links the two names also links their respective locations — that is, the local river, the name of which stems from Old English *gyse-sic* and refers to 'the gushing stream'. These places are found recorded as Gyssic in the tenth century, Gessic in Domesday, Gussich All Saints in 1245, and Gussich St Michael in 1297.

At Gussage St Michael we find names such as Week Street Down, itself from a Week Street mentioned in Anglo-Saxon records. This has nothing to do with a length of time, nor is it a mis-spelt 'weak'; this comes from Old English *wic*, a term used to describe

Milepost at Godmanstone.

Smith's Arms, Godmanstone —
England's smallest inn.

a 'specialised farm', and almost always that speciality is simply dairy produce. Ogden Down Farm also had its speciality, the name coming from Old English *hogg* and not, as it might seem, a piggery but one which raised 'young sheep', thus clearly for meat more than wool. Canada Farm and Doctor's Farm are named from the country and the occupation, but why they were chosen is not known.

Gussage All Saints has Bidcombe Mill, a name associated with John de Bitcombe and Robert Bitcombe who were here in the fourteenth and fifteenth centuries respectively. Bowerswain Farm is a name thatis corruption of Old English *bar fenn*, 'the marshland of the boar'. However, the 's' here may be posessive, in which case the first element is a personal name Bar, from 'boar' and used as a nickname.

Brockington Farm refers to 'the farmstead associated with the dwellers on the brook'. Harley Down points to the soil when it is defined as 'the hill at the hard clearing'. With a name meaning 'Leofwaru's woodland clearing' comes the name of Loverley Farm. Wyke Farm features the element *wic*, an Old English term for a 'specialised farm', and one that invariably refers to a dairy farm. Custard Hill is from *cot stow*, which is understood as describing 'the collection of cottages', while Ton Bridge is likely describing 'the bridge belonging to the village'.

Chapter 8

Halstock to Hurn

HALSTOCK

The earliest record of this name is as Halganstoke in 998. This is from the Old English combination of *halig-stoc* and refers to 'the outlying place belonging to a religious community'.

HAMMOON

Recorded as Hame in 1086, this name comes from Old English *hamm* and, while it has several meanings, is here seen as 'water meadow' or 'place in a river bend'. The addition comes from the manor being held by the Moion family, and indeed are recorded as being here in the Domesday record even if their name does not become a part of the place name until Hamme Moun in 1280.

Local names include Tan Hill Copse, a name from Old English *tan hyll* and which refers to 'the hill with a twig or shoot', one which would have stood out against the skyline making it instantly recognisable.

HAMPRESTON

A name recorded as simply Hame in 1086, the addition is not seen until 1244 as Hamme Preston. The original name is from Old English *hamm* or 'river meadow', while the later addition is from *preost tun* or 'the farmstead associated with the priests'.

Fern Down is from fergen or 'the wooded hill'; Hillamsland has a complex history but is unlikely to be little different from 'the dwellers of the enclosure at the hill'; Longham speaks of 'the long hemmed in land' and refers to the spit of land formed by a bend in the river; Ameysford Road is associated with the family of John and Roger Arney, here in 1598; and Pilford Lane leads to 'the ford marked by a stake'.

HAMWORTHY

A place name found as Hamme in 1236 and as the modern form in 1463. Here the two elements *hamm* and *worthig* come together to describe 'the hemmed in land with an enclosure'.

Rock Lea is derived from 'the reedy bank at the spring or stream', and is seen as the name of a Bridge, Hill, Point and River. From Old English *thyrelung* comes the name of Turlin Farm, a word meaning literally 'piercing' and describing a deep and curving valley'.

The close proximity to the sea is recognised by the Yachtsman Inn.

HANFORD

A name recorded exactly as the modern form in Domesday, although in the intervening years we find Haunford, Hamford, Hampford, Enforde, Hanneford, Honforde, and Handford. All these records point to a likely origin of *han ford* and describe 'the ford at the stone', although it may be *heah ford* meaning 'the high ford'. Either way, this was doubtless of great importance and had been used for many years as indicated by the name of Holloway Lane in neighbouring Shillingstone, this telling us that this path had been worn to a hollow through constant use.

Locally we find Bournes Barn and Great Bournes, which may have been deliberately adjusted by the Victorians who considered the name of Great Bones, as recorded in 1869, to be inappropriate. This name must come from the Roman villa discovered here in 1860 when human remains were also discovered. Whether the villa and the cemetery were contemporary is still a matter for debate. Nutcombe Wood is not from the toponomy here, but it was brought here by Richard Nutcomb who married into the daughter of Robert Seymer, lord of this manor, in 1692.

HAYDON

A name thatmeans 'the place at the hill (or down) where hay is made'. This comes from Old English *heg dun* and is recorded as Heydone in 1163.

Coach Hill Wood has nothing to do with coaches or, oddly enough, any hill. A document dated 1677 speaks of the Tenement called Coxalls, while an earlier record associates this place with the family of William le Cok and thus should be seen as 'the nook of land associated with the Cook family'.

HAZELBURY BRYAN

The addition here, first seen in the record of 1547 as Hasibere Bryan, refers to the Bryene family who were known to be here in the fourteenth century. Previously this is seen as Hasebere in 1201, from Old English *haesel-bearu* and refers to this as 'the grove of hazel'.

Here we find Droop Farm, a corruption of the common Old English *thorp*, or 'outlying or secondary settlement'. Kingston is easy to see as 'the farmstead of the king', and indeed in 1275 this was recorded as once held by Richard de Hasilbere for King John.

Other names include Wonston, which was 'Wulfmaer's farmstead'; Woodrow Farm tells us it was situated 'at the row of trees'; Frizells Hill has three Old English elements, *fyrs*, *hyll* and *hyll*, and describes itself as 'the hill where furze grows'; Locketts Farm remembers the family of John Lockett, here by 1386; what was 'the road leading to the market town' is today known as Partway Lane; Pyle *wella* is named from 'the well or spring marked by stakes'; Silly Hill is probably from *sele* or 'the copse of willow trees'; Stivvicks Bridge unites the elements *stig* and *byrde* and describes 'the border path' that runs along the tributary of the River Lydden; and Stut Lane, from *steort* or 'the projecting piece of land'.

The Antelope makes an attractive recognisable symbol and name for a pub, which is why it was chosen as an heraldic image. It is representative of many, including Henry IV, Henry V, Henry VI, the dukes of Bedford, and dukes of Gloucester.

HERMITAGE

A name which has existed for centuries and has changed hardly at all, Hermitage began as a small hut or shelter where a pious individual or group lived in virtual solitude in order to devote their lives to God.

HIGHCLIFFE

A very simple and self-explanatory name which is not seen until 1759 as High Clift and does indeed mean the '(place at) the high cliff'. Earlier a record of 1610 gives this as Black Cliffe, also a name of obvious meaning and one that was probably changed deliberately.

The Hinton Oak takes the common reference to an obvious landmark, and there is no tree larger than the oak, this one by Hinton Wood Avenue.

HIGHER ANSTY

A common name, from Old English *anstig*, 'the narrow or lonely track', Higher Ansty has an obvious addition.

HILFIELD

From Old English *hyll feld* and recorded as Hylfelde in 934, this is 'the open land by a hill'.

HILTON

Domesday records this as Eltone, which is significantly different from the modern form and may suggest the origin of Old English *hielde tun* and 'the farmstead on a slope'. The alternative here is *helde tun* or 'the farmstead where tansy grows', a plant that has been cultivated since the days of the Greek Empire and used for medicinal purposes.

Aller Farm was 'at the alder trees'; Higher Ansty and Little Ansty take their names from anstiga and describing 'the path for one, a narrow track'; the name Hartfoot Lane tells of 'the highway'; the 'hawthorn clearing' is now Hatherley Farm; Newton Farm may be 'the new farmstead' but it has not been 'new' since at least 1400; Chilmore was 'the moorland given over to the younger sons'; and the name of Rawlsbury Camp is an Iron Age fort which describes itself as 'the ringed fortification'.

HINTON ST MARY

A very common place name from Old English *hean tun* and referring to 'the high farm', although this is understood as more often being the principal of chief farm rather than any elevated position. Documented evidence of the evolution of this name is seen by Hamtune in 944, Haintone in 1086, and as Hinton Marye in 1627, this latest example pointing to its possession by the Abbey of St Mary at Shaftesbury.

Locally we find Yewstock, a macabre name from Old English *heafod-stocc* and describing 'the post on which the head of a criminal was displayed'. Cut Mill Lane refers to 'the water channel, mill race' feeding the mill mentioned in Domesday. Marriage Lane may make a good location for a wedding photograph today, but historically it comes from *mere brycg* and refers to 'the ridge where mares were grazed'.

HINTON MARTELL

As with the previous name, this is 'the high or chief farmstead', with the addition of the lords of the manor in the thirteenth century, the Martell family. The name is recorded as Hintone in 1086 and Hineton Martel in 1226.

Local names include Woodcutts Farm, a name which began as *wudu cot*, or 'the cottages in the wood'; Emley Lane ran alongside the *efn leah* or 'level woodland clearing'; Gaunt's Common must refer to John of Gaunt, Duke of Lancaster 1372-99, who held land and was granted a fair here in 1368; Pill Well speaks of 'the pool in a stream'; Piper's Hill was named from the family of Roger Pipere, here by 1332; and Uppingtown is a modern form of *upp in tun*, or 'the highest part of the settlement'.

HINTON PARVA

Recorded as Parva Hyneton in 1285, this 'high or chief farmstead' features the Latin addition of parva, or 'little', which was how the place was listed from the late fourteenth century with Middle English *lytel*.

Minor place names here include Stanbridge, which certainly comes from *stan brycg* but may have referred to a raised causeway rather than a stone bridge, for the road still passes across low-lying, potentially marshy ground.

HOLME (EAST & WEST)

A name from Old English *helgn* and referring to the '(place at) the holly trees', while the additions speak for themselves. This name is found as Holne in 1086, with Estholn and Westholn in 1228.

Road sign at the entrance to Holnest village.

At East Holme we find Battle Plain, which marks the site of a battle during the English Civil War. Job's Plain was associated with tenant Henry Jobbe in 1340. Monk's Pond is the place where the old fish pond was stocked to provide food for the men in Holm Priory. Three Lords Barrow refers to the tumulus that stands at the boundary of no less than four parishes, and doubtless at the time the name originated it was held by three different manors.

HOLNEST

A name that is clearly similar to the previous entry, here the same Old English *holegn* is followed by *hyrst* from the same language. This is recorded as Holeherst in 1185 and describes 'the wooded hill where holly grows'.

Local names include Boys Hill, named from the family of Adam and William Boye who are documented here in a document of 1314. Cancer Drove is a lane that comes from Old English *canne scega* and describes 'the hollow in the copse'. Berkeley's Plantation was associated with Agnes and Richard Berkeleford in 1327; Bunter's Copse was home to the family of Richard Bunter in 1620; Davis's Plantation is a reminder that Mark Davis bought this manor in the early nineteenth century; and Dyer's Farm reminds us that Margaret Dyer's family were living here in 1599.

William Gordon held the neighbouring Leweston estate until 1802 — this name is discuseed under its own entry — and he is commemorated by the name of Gordon's Gorse. Mackey's Copse is derived from *mearc haeg* and describes 'the boundary enclosure' and this place is on the parish boundary. Osmond Farm reminds us that John Osmonde was here in 1474 and William Osmunde in 1542.

The church at Holnest.

HOLT

A name found quite often and usually in combination with another element, but the meaning is always 'the thicket'. Interestingly, records of this name show it did once have another element, as seen by Holte in 1372 and as Winburneholt in 1305. The addition is from this place once being the possession of Wimbourne Minster.

Local names include Bothenwood, a name featuring two Old English elements *bothen wudu* and probably referring to 'the wood where rosemary, darnel, or thyme is collected'. However, the earliest surviving record of this place name dates from the early fourteenth century, a period when Old English was giving way to Middle English. The word *bothen* in Middle English referred to the plant 'corn marigold', while there was also *botham* or *bothen*, dialect words used around Dorset and Hampshire also referring to the 'corn marigold'. Lack of any earlier record before the fourteenth century does not point to any particular origin.

Grange Farm is derived from *grange* 'the outlying farm'; Honeybrook Farm here comes from Old English *hunig broc* 'the brook where honey is collected'; Linen Hill Farm describes 'the hill where flax is grown'; Mannington is 'the farmstead associated with a man called Manna'; Petersham Farm began as 'Peohtric's homestead'; Uddens House takes a place name from 'Udda's place', although it could be from *wudu laes* 'the woodland pasture'; and Barewood comes from *bearu wudu*, 'the grove in a wood'.

Bowering's Water is a ford associated with William Bowring, here in 1664; Bower's Farm reminds us of the family of Benjamin Bower, here by 1763; Early's Farm was associated with thirteenth century landholder the Earl of Leicester; God's Blessing Farm gave a name to God's Blessing Lane and refers to very productive or scenic land; Humphrey's Copse is named from the family of Nicholas Humfrey, here by 1591; Organ lawn seems unlikely to refer to the musical instrument, more likely from origan meaning 'wild marjoram or pennyroyal'; from *trendel* comes Trendell's Copse and describes 'a circular area'; Summerlug Hill is from *lug* 'a perch used in summer', a region and while Daffodil Copse may bring to mind the popular spring flower, it is recorded as Daffys Coppice in 1840 and is almost certainly from a surname.

HOLTON HEATH

The addition here is self-explanatory and required for a common name. Recorded as Holtone in 1086 and from Old English *hol-tun* this is 'the farmstead in a hollow' Alternatively the first element here is Old English *holt* and describing this as 'the farmstead of the wood', early forms are insufficently diverse to show which is the true origin.

HOLWELL

No record of this name survives from earlier than that of Holewala in 1188. It seems this comes from Old English *hol walu* and referring to this as 'the bank in the hollow'.

HOLWORTH

A name similar to the previous entry and from Old English *hol worth*. It is recorded as Holewertthe in 934 and Holverde in 1086, this tells us it was 'the enclosure in a hollow'.

Local names include Buckshaw Farm and Lower Buckshaw, which share a name from Middle English *bugge* and Old English *sceaga* and describe 'the hobgoblin wood'. Cornford Bridge was built at the 'ford by the mill', while the names of Sandhills and Woodbridge speak for themselves. The copse called Ladysmith was clearly named to commemorate the relief of that beseiged town in 1900, a major point in the Boer War.

HOOKE

A place name meaning 'the place in a hook of land', say a loop in a river or a natural boundary of hills or even vegetation. This comes from Old English *hoc*, but is not unlike the Norman French *Lahoc* seen in Domesday, indeed only the feminine definite article la distinguishes one from the other. Clearly, with the two languages quite different branches of the same Indo-European group, this is a term used since the times when the nomadic peoples first travelled Europe anywhere from the 4,000 BC to 10,000 BC and even before.

It should be noted that the Proto-Indo-European language is unknown, merely seen by comparing similar words from later known languages be they in current use or not.

It has been argued that no such language existed and that simple single syllable terms, such as hot, cold, big, dry, wet, hard, etc, are likely to produce similarites between languages — there are few words and fewer sounds to work with and thus similarites are inevitable. Furthermore, doubtless there were innumerable variations of the same theme; however, there must have been a first spoken word, the first use of grammar, the first name and the first sentence. In each case, someone had to speak it, and in later years, each milestone was repeated when the written forms appeared. Language would have appeared in several places, much the same as writing appeared in several places in quite different ways and thus came about quite independently. It is virtually impossible to see languages evolving quite independently to such a degree, as there just were not enough cultures to produce such a variety in such a short space of time.

HORTON

Listed as Hortun in 1033 and Hortune in 1086, this comes from Old English *horu-tun* and describes 'the dirty or muddy farmstead'.

Brickplace Copse was where bricks were made from the eighteenth century; Doe's Hatch was 'the floodgate or hatch frequented by does'; Priors Copse is a reminder of the Benedictine abbey founded in the tenth century which was later a priory, these lands are also commemorated by Manor Farm; Old Read's Copse takes the name of the family of Robert le Rede, here by 1332; while Redman's Hill refers to John Redman's family, here in the seventeenth century.

HURN

Domesday suggests this place name is Herne, a fair phonetic representation of the Old English *hyrne* and also seen in the pronunciation of the modern form. Yet there is also a similarity to the word 'horn', a good description of the shape of a place name referring to the 'angle or corner of land'.

Chapter 9

Ibberton to Iwerne

IBBERTON

Domesday gives this place name as Abrisetone in 1086, and this name comes from a Saxon personal name and Old English *ing tun*, and describing this as 'the farmstead associated with a man called Eadbeorht'.

Aplin's Heath remembers the family of Roger Aplin, here by 1664; George Harvey Baker was responsible for Baker's Folly around 1870; Kitford is 'the ford frequented by kites'; Ryalls Lane ran alongside 'the hill where rye was grown'; while Stibles Lane is undoubtedly a surname, although no record of such survives.

The Crown Inn shows an early landlord or owner was a patriot and, more importantly, a Royalist.

ICKNEILD WAY

A name that refers to an ancient trackway linking Dorset with Norfolk. Often said to be a Roman road and thus named from a Latin term, the earliest record we have is as Icenhylte in 903. It has been adopted for the Roman road from Bourton on the Water in Gloucestershire to near Rotherham in Yorkshire and, while it has also been seen as Ryknild Street, was not named by the Romans for it was never seen by this name until the twelfth century. The origins of this name are unclear and any suggestions would be speculative, although it may be related to the Iceni tribe who lived around the area corresponding to modern Norfolk roughly from AD 100 to 100 BC, the similarity may be coincidental, for the trackway certainly existed centuries and possibly millennia prior to this.

IPPLEDEN

Listings of this name include Iplanpen and Ipelanpaenne in the tenth century and Iplepene in Domesday. The name is of Old English origin and refers to 'Ipa's pen or fold'.

ISLE OF PORTLAND

A name that comes from Old English *port land* meaning 'the farmstead of the harbour'. It is recorded as Port in the ninth century, Portlande in 862, and Porland in 1086.

Streets here include Avalanche Road, named after the Avalanche, a ship that sank off the island on the night of 13 September 1877. The vessel was bound for Wellington, New Zealand, when it was hit amidships by the American vessel Forest. Both vessels sank inside three minutes, resulting in the loss of ninety-six lives. Nine of the twenty-five American sailors survived, as did three of the thirty-four crew aboard the Avalanche. None of the sixty-three passengers made it, most of whom were colonists returning to New Zealand. For days afterwards bodies were being washed up on the shore of the Isle of Portland, including whole families.

Clement's Lane reminds us of Nicholas Clement, who was here by 1323. Chesil Beach comes from Old English *cisel bece* and tells of 'the shingle beach', a line of pebbles which have been dropped here by the currents over thousands of years and now measure some sixteen miles in length and still growing. Fortuneswell can still be seen as being 'the lucky spring or well' but just why it should be described as being fortunate or lucky is a mystery. Reford puts together Old English *horn* and Middle English *riff* to describe 'the headland with a fissure, a rift'. *Fergen geat*, or 'the wooded hill with a gap or gaps', is today marked as Verne Yeates.

Other names include Wakeham meaning 'the watch point valley'; Alma Cottages are named from one of the most famous battles of the Crimean War; Fancy Beach is taken from a surname; Nicodemus Knob is a column of rock formed from quarrying, used as a navigation point it is unclear how it acquired such a name; while the name of Pennsylvania Castle was built in 1800 by John Penn, governor of Portland and grandson of William Penn, the man who founded Pennsylvania, USA and after whom it is named.

Pulpit Rock is a local name for a rock which does indeed resemble that part of the church; Blow Hole is a cave feature where the sea water broke through a hole in the roof of the cave and very reminiscent of a whale, while there is also a name of Cave Hole which may or may not refer to the same feature. Silklake Quarries is derived from Silk Lane, nothing to do with the coveted cloth but from Old English *seoluc* and describing 'a gully, drain'.

A couple of amusing names include Shepherd's Dinner Quarry, named after Robert le Shepherde who was here in 1323, the addition of the meal seems to have been deliberate and without any etymological value. From Old English *suth cumb* and describing 'the southern valley' is now known as Suckthumb Quarry.

ISLE OF PURBECK

A name found in 948 as Purbicinga and in 1086 as Porbi, this name comes from Old English *pur bic* and probably telling of this being 'the beak shaped ridge frequented by bittern or snipe'.

IWERNE (COURTNEY, SHROTON & MINSTER)

Clearly, the additions here are to distinguish one from the other, for these places are quite near one another. Records show these places as Ywern in 877, with Werne and Evneministre in 1086, names which come from a Celtic river name Iwerne, associated with all three and meaning 'the yew tree river', or possibly an unknown Celtic goddess. The addition of Minster is from Old English *mynster* and is 'the church of the monastery', which refers to its possession by Shaftesbury Abbey. The addition of the Courtenay family, lords of the manor in the thirteenth century, is the clear basis for another addition, but, as the record of 1403 shows, this place is known by two names and was then listed as Iwerne Corteney alias Shyrevton. This alternative is from Old English *scir refa tun* and tells it was 'the sheriff's estate'. Hence Irwene Courtney is also Irwene Shroton, and officially today still known as both names.

Minor names include Farrington Farm, a modern form of what had always been *fearn dun* or 'the fearn-covered hill'. Ranston describes 'Randulf's *tun* or farmstead'; Tray Town is a name found on the parish boundary, which probably comes from troy town, a common name given to 'a maze'; Lady Meadow was land associated with the Free School here in 1838, and this place of education was established by the lady of the manor, Dame Elizabeth Freke, in 1705.

Peggs Farm and Peggs Mill Bridge share a surname recorded in 1317 when the mill was worked by John and Robert le Peg. Freak's Coppice is derived from *freakes*, which is another word for a 'coppice', thus the family name of Thomas and Robert Freke, here in 1578, are derived from the place name. However, Fry's Coppice does take a family name, that of Francis Fry who held this manor during the reign of Elizabeth I.

At Iwerne Shroton the national sport of any summer we may enjoy is recognised by the local pub. The Cricketers is a name that enables sign painters to depict that quintessential village scene.

Chapter 10

Kimmeridge to Knighton

KIMMERIDGE

The first element shown by Domesday's record of Cameric can be discounted, thus we look at the listing of Kimerich in 1212. This has two possible origins and is either a personal name as 'Cyma's strip of land', or this is Old English *cyme ric* referring to 'the convenient strip of land'.

Local names include Smedmore House, itself from a place name from Old English *smethe mor*, or 'the smooth moorland' — that is, a landscape unbroken by trees or rocks. Clavel Tower and Clavell's Hard are named after a member of the Clavell family, with John Clavyle being the earliest in 1423, but likely refers to Sir William Clavel who tried to establish an alum industry here in the seventeenth century. Swalland Farm comes from Old English *swan land*, 'the land of the herdsmen'.

KINGSTON LACY

A common name indeed, one which comes from Old English *cyning tun* and meaning 'the king's estate', which is here given the second defining element courtesy of the de Lacy family who held this manor from the thirteenth century. The name is recorded as Kingestune in 1170 and as Kynggestone Lucy in 1319.

KINGSTON RUSSELL

As if to prove that this is, as stated in the previous entry, a common name here is another *cyning tun*. This 'king's estate' was held by John Russel in 1212, this being an Old French surname meaning 'red'.

KINGTON MAGNA

As with the previous name, this is 'the royal farmstead' from Old English *cyne tun*. Here the suffix comes from Latin *magna* meaning 'great'.

The names of Higher Nyland and Lower Nyland share a common origin, the meaning of which is clearly *atten ieg land*, which is almost self-explanatory if pronounced 'at an island' and seen as 'the dry ground in a marsh'. Breach Lane gets its name from *braec*, describing the adjoining 'land newly broken up for cultivation'. Bye Farm is from *byge* or 'corner, bend', and the place does stand at a sharp angle in the parish boundary. Although named Five Bridges, there has only ever been one here; however, in the sixteenth century it is noted that Five Bridges was comprised of five main arches. Harpitts Lane and Harpitts Farm come from 'the grey pit', while Juan's Lane has nothing to do with a Spanish gent but is a corruption of the Jones family name, William was the earliest recorded here in 1664.

KINSON

Listed as Kinestanston in 1238, this name speaks of 'Cynestan's farmstead', with the Saxon personal name followed by the common Old English element tun.

Here we find names such as Cudnell, 'Cuda's hill or nook of land'; Ensbury Farm was probably 'Aegen's fortified place'; Bankes Heath is named after the family who were lords of this manor from the mid-seventeenth century; Duke's Coppice is not a reference to a member of the nobility but refers to the family of Walter le Douk who were here by 1327; and Wallis Down is a reminder of the family of Richard Waleys, here in 1332.

KNIGHTON (WEST)

Another fairly common name which, as we would expect, comes from Old English *cniht-tun* but does not come refer to a knight, which we would envisage in the modern day. Instead this is 'the farmstead of the young thanes or retainers', being recorded as Chenistone in 1086, with an obvious addition.

Higher Lewell Farm and Lower Lewell Farm share a common origin from *hleow wella*, or quite literally 'the well spring with a shelter', hence the 'well with an easily removable cover'. Huck Barrow describes 'the barrow at the corner of land', and here there is an historical parish boundary.

Chapter 11

Langton Herring to Lytchett

LANGTON HERRING

A name found across much of England and, almost without exception, coming from Old English *lang-tun* or 'the long farmstead'. So common is this place name that additions are almost obligatory; the Harang family were lords of this manor in the thirteenth century. The name is recorded as Langetone in 1086 and Langeton Heryng in 1336.

LANGTON LONG BLANDFORD

A name recorded as simply Bleneford in 1086, it had become Longa Bladeneford by 1179. This is another 'ford where bray or gudgeon are found', and the additions are not the same but refer to different places; 'long Blandford' differentiates from other Blandfords nearby and Langton or 'the long farmstead' was originally a neighbouring manor.

This place has many records and could justifiably lay claim to the most recorded parish name in Dorset, while also having more potential additions than any other place name in the county. In 1548, we find Langeton Boteler, a reference to John le Botiller whose family held this manor by 1280; in 1421, Langeton Latyle refers to the family of John de la Tylle; Blaneford Michael Belet reminds us of Michael Belet, here in 1216, with a later record of Emma Belet in 1254; and Gylden Langton in 1546 and Langton Gundon in 1664 both refer to the family of Henry le Gildene or Elizabeth de Gulden, both of whom were here in the fourteenth century.

Littleton Farm is named from 'the small farmstead'; Londonderry was transferred here by someone from Northern Ireland. However, Scotland is more likely to be from Old English *scot* or 'taxable land'; Snow's Down is named from the family of George Snow, who held this manor by 1800; and Lophill Farm, which comes from *lobb*, literally 'something heavy', with *hyll* and understood as meaning 'the place at the steep slope', i.e. difficult to get up to.

LANGTON MATRAVERS

As with the previous name, this is 'the long farmstead'. Here the addition comes form the Mautravers family who were lords of this manor in the thirteenth century. The name is recorded as Langeton in 1165 and Langeton Mawtravers in 1428.

Here we find minor names such as Acton, not the normal 'oak tree farmstead' but from Old English *tacca-tun* and describing 'the farmstead where young sheep are reared'. Durnford Drove refers to 'the field track through the hidden ford'; Knitson was earlier the name of a farm and which comes from 'the farmstead of a man called Cnihtwine'; Lesson tells of 'the farmstead of a man called Leofsige'; and what began as 'Willic's woodland' is marked on maps as Wilkswood Farm.

Chillmark comes from Old English *cegel mearc*, or 'the boundary marked by poles'. Putlake Farm lies next to 'the goblin's stream', which may not refer to an impish sprite but remarks on how the stream behaves mischieviously by flooding the farm without warning.

Dancing Ledge is an abandoned cliff-side quarry, so called because the way the waves break over the ledge, within is a depression known as the Bathing Pool and which fills with water. To reach these two places one needs to slide across a small cliff-top quarry covered by scree, a place known as Scratch Arse.

LEIGH

With the earliest record from 1242 as Lega, this name features one of the most common elements in English place name. However, *leah*, meaning 'woodland clearing', is almost always found as a suffix.

LEWESTON

First found in 1145 as Luistuna, there are later records of Lewestun, Loueston, Leuston, Lewiston and Leuweston in the thirteenth century alone. This name features a Saxon personal name and Old English *tun* and refers to 'the farmstead of a man called Leofwig'.

LILLINGTON

Records of this name include Lilletone in 1166 and Lulinton in 1200; this name comes from 'the farmstead associated with a man called Lylla' and features a Saxon personal name with the Old English *ing tun*.

Bailey Ridge Farm and Bailey Ridge Lane was 'the ridge of land within a bailliff's jurisdiction' and which points to this being held by John Streeche in neighbouring Holnest and was taxed as if this place was a part of Holnest. Higher and Lower Stockbridge Farms share a common etymology in *stoccen brycg* and describe 'the bridge made of logs'.

LITTLE BREDY

Listed as Litebride in 1086, this place name takes the name of the River Bride, itself a Celtic river name meaning 'gushing or surging stream'. The addition, from Old English *lytel* meaning 'little', is to distinguish it from the earlier settlement of Long Bredy.

The Rose & Crown at Longburton.

LITTON CHENEY

A place name not seen before 1204 when it is documented as Lideton, this name comes from Old English *hlyde-tun* and describes 'the farmstead by a noisy stream', with the addition referring to the fourteenth-century lords of the manor the Cheyne family.

LODERS

Originally the name of the river here and a place name recorded as Lodre in Domesday. While the river name is now known as the River Asker, previously it was known by this name, which explains why the place name means 'the pool of the stream'.

LONG BREDY

Again, a name that comes from the Celtic river name of Bride, or the 'gushing or surging stream'. The addition, of obvious meaning, is derived from the Old English *lang*; the place is recorded as Bridian in 987 and Langebride in 1086.

LONGBURTON

From Old English *burh tun* or 'the farmstead with a fortification', this represents one of the most common place names in the country and one which is recorded as Burton in 1244 and Langebourton in 1460. The addition, also from Old English, is *lang* and describes this as a 'settlement of a long shape'. There is also a Little Burton, which was once also known as West Burton — both additions are self-explanatory.

Street Lane marks the site of a former Roman road; Bradford Lane marked the site of 'the broad ford'; Quarr Shrub and Quarry Lane both remember quarries that were once worked here.

LONGFLEET

Recorded as Langeflete in 1230 and Langflete iuxta Mare in 1463, this name is derived from Old English *lang fleot* and describing 'the long inlet or creek'. Furthermore, this term is used to describe a tidal creek, a fact emphasised by the fifteenth-century record with Latin mare meaning 'the sea'.

Other names found here are Sterte from *steort*, or 'tail of land'; Tatnam Farm speaks of 'Totta's homestead'; Ladies Walking Ford is a very shallow river crossing, passable by a lady in those long dresses; and Turbary Allotment tells us it was where peat was dug for fuel.

LULWORTH (EAST & WEST)

Domesday records this name as Lulvorde and means 'Lulla's enclosure', with the Saxon personal name preceding Old English *worth*. The additions of East and West are self-explanatory.

At East Lulworth is a region known as Arish Mell, which seems to refer to a 'rounded feature' in the gap in the chalk cliffs. Flower's Barrow is from Old English *flor beorg* and literally 'the floor by the barrow', the floor being a tesselated pavement left over from the Roman occupation. Botany Bay is a remoteness name, suggesting this corner of the parish seems as far away as Australia.

West Lulworth has Belhuish Farm, the 'hide of land associated with a woman called Beaghild'; Burgate Farm could come from several origins, the most likely speaking of 'the brown gate or path'; Bacon Bluff and Bacon Hole are cliff features said to have been given this name because of their streaky appearance;

Offshore rocks and other coastal features here are known by an assortment of names: there is the Bull and the Blind Cow, although the reason behind this is unknown; the Man o' War is said to resemble an early nineteenth-century warship, while Man o' War Cove is named from the rock; Church Rock has no clear etymology; Scratchy Bottom sees an uneven valley facing out to sea; Sea Horse is a rock which has no resemblance to the fish; Stair Hole is a steep-sided hole, which would be like climbing a long staircase; Pinion Rock is said to resemble a pinion or 'bird's wing'; while the list would not be complete without Smugglers Cave, an out of the way cave system which certainly fits the romantic notion of a secret way used by smugglers.

A road sign at Lyon's Gate.

LYDDEN (RIVER)

This is a Celtic river name and descibes itself as 'the broad one'.

LYDLINCH

A place name recorded as Lidelinz in 1182 and where the first element represents the River Lydden and is followed by Old English *hlinc*. Thus this place is 'the ridge or bank by the Lydden'.

Blackrow Farm takes its name from Old English *blaec raw* and describes 'the dark-coloured row of trees'; Holebrook Farm is situated close to the 'stream running in a hollow'; Plumber Farm comes from *plume bearu*, 'the woodland grove where plum trees grow'; from *hreod mor*, or 'the marshy land where reeds grow', comes the name of Rodmore Farm; and Salkeld Bridge was named after the Salkeld family who held lands here from the eighteenth century.

While Stock Gaylard tells us it was 'the outlying farmstead' and seemingly associated with the Gaylard or Galliard family, there is no record of any such family ever being here. There are records of similar names in nearby parishes, such as Nicholas Callard and Richard Coulard at Up Cerne in 1332 and William Coulard of Folke in 1436.

LYME REGIS

As with the previous name, the basis for this place name is the local river. Recorded as Lim in 724, Lime in 1086, and Lyme Regis as early as 1285, this Celtic river name comes from the simple description of 'stream' and is joined by Latin *regis* from the thirteenth century, referring to it being held by 'the king'.

Local pubs, as we would expect, are keen to reflect the location by the sea. The Harbour Inn and the Rock Point Inn are coastal features, while the Pilot Boat Inn is named from the men whose local knowledge enabled larger vessels to be guided through a maze of unseen underwater hazards, this was in the days before pinpoint satellite navigation or any up-to-date map of shifting sandbanks or mud.

The Cobb Arms is not a family, and those who know Lyme Regis will be aware this is the name given to the harbour wall that protects and forms the safe haven, which is the harbour. Even those who have never been to the port may have unknowingly seen or read about the Cobb. An important place since the thirteenth century, this harbour wall has been damaged and rebuilt several times, Lyme Regis being an important port and larger than Liverpool up to the end of the eighteenth century, when the ships literally outgrew the place.

The Cobb is an important part of Jane Austen's novel Persuasion and is one of the most memorable parts of the film The French Lieutenant's Woman, while Sir Richard Spencer RN developed the basic technology behind lifeboats here from 1824.

LYTCHETT (MATRAVERS & MINSTER)

The earliest forms of these place names are as Lichet in 1086, Lichet Mautrauers in 1280 and Licheminster in 1244. This is one of the few place names that features two Celtic elements and is not a river or hill name and features *led-ced* or 'the grey wood'. Two places in such close proximity require additions and are here seen as referring to the Maltrauers family and from Old English *mynster* or 'the large church'.

At Lytchett Matravers we find local names such as Brock Hill, where 'badgers are seen'; Cuzenage Coppice literally describes the 'fraud, deception' and, as it stands near the boundary, quite obviously refers to a disputed boundary or marker; Luscombe Wood is the 'valley with a pig sty'; and while Warmwell Farm is officially defined as 'the warm spring or stream' it should probably be seen as 'less cold' by comparison.

Pubs here include the Rose & Crown, the former representing England and the latter the monarchy, showing this person was a patriot and a royalist. The Chequers Inn is one of the oldest of pub names, being around during the days of the Roman Empire. In early days, innkeepers invariably had two careers, most notably a moneyer. The chequerboard was hung outside and conveyed two messages: the board was used to play a boardgame and also used to indicate a financier. This has echoed down to the present day in the office of Chancellor of the Exchequer.

Lytchett Minster has Bere Farm, either *baer*, 'pasture', or *bearu*, 'woodland'; Newton Farm may have originally been 'the new farmstead', but this is more likely to have been taken from a family name; Slepe is 'the muddy, slippery place'; Peter's Finger is most often said to be a corruption of 'St Peter ad Vincula', this Latin dedication referring to St Peter in Chains, and this place name is also taken for the pub, the St Peter's Finger.

Chapter 12

Maiden Newton to Mudeford

MAIDEN NEWTON

A name recorded as Newetone in 1086 and as Maydene Neweton in 1316. The basic name is *niwe tun*, or 'the new farmstead', although as it was known as such at the time of Domesday in the late eleventh century and perhaps we should see this as 'newer farmstead' in comparison with some nearby place. The addition means 'associated with the maidens' and probably shows some early connection of this place with nuns.

MANNINGTON

A name recorded in 1248 as Manitone, this place name is derived from a Saxon personal name with Old English *treow*. Together they tell of this being 'the tree of a man called Manna'.

MANSTON

Here is a place name meaning 'the farmstead of a man called Mann', with the Saxon personal name followed by Old English tun. The name is recorded in Domesday in 1086 as Manestone.

In 1664, Coles Close was associated with Richard Cole, John Fry is recorded as being at Frys Meadow, Goddens was home to Thomas Godwin, and Philip Nicholas was living near Nicholas's Wood.

MAPPERTON

Listings of this place name begin with Domesday and Malperetone. This is from Old English *mapuldor-tun* and describes 'the farmstead where maple trees are found'.

MAPPOWDER

An unusual name, first seen in Domesday in 1086 as Mapledre. Whilst this may seem to have little more than a passing resemblance to previous name, they both feature the same Old English element *mapuldor*; indeed this is the basis for for both versions and describes the '(place at) the maple trees'.

Minor place names here include Boywood Farm, which is probably 'the wood associated with the boys or servants' rather than 'Boia's wood'. Devils Wood is recorded as Evills Wood in the seventeenth century, this earlier record shows no link to anything sinister but points to Old English *aewiell*, 'the source of the stream', and there is a stream that rises here. Hammond Street Farm reminds us that the family of Walter Hammond were here by 1297.

MARGARET MARSH

A name recorded as Margaretysmerschchurche in 1395, a name which residents must be thankful is not in use today; however, the early nineteenth century record of St Margaret's Marsh explains clearly the origin of the name.

Gore Farm describes 'the triangular area of land'; Jopp's Farm is named from the family of Geoffrey Jop and Juliana Joppe, who were here by 1291, and the name was also applied to Jopp's Ford, which no longer appears on maps.

MARNHULL

Here a Saxon personal name is suffixed by Old English *hyll* and tells us of 'the hill of a man called Mearna'. The earliest surviving record of this name is as Marnhulle from 1267.

Burton Street leads to 'the farmstead associated with a fortification', while Marnhull Ham refers to 'the homestead in the river bend' but was earlier known as Burtlingham in the fourteenth century, a name describing 'the river meadow of the people of Burton'. Moor Court Farm and Moorside describe 'the marshy land', Nash Court comes from *atten aesc* court, or the 'large house at the ash tree'.

Ram's Hill has nothing to do with male sheep and nor does it refer to wild garlic from *hramsa*, but is *rum hyll* and describes 'the roomy hill'. Thornton Farm speaks of 'the thorny farmstead'; Yardgrove Farm has long been 'the grove where rods are obtained' and used for building; and Walton is found several times, with a single origin in *wealh tun*, or 'the farmstead of the Welshmen'. Lymburgh's Farm is either 'the hill of lime trees' from *lind beorg* or perhaps stems from *lin beorg* in which case it would be 'the hill where flax is grown'.

Breach Farm was originally 'the land newly broken for cultivation' and, while every field starts with breaking up compacted soil, it does show that this place was farmed later than other parts of the settlement. Fillymead refers to itself as 'the clearing where hay was cut', and Hingarston describes 'the farmstead of grass, pasture'. Hussey's Copse is a reminder of George Hussey, whose family bought this manor in 1651.

Sackmore Lane comes from *sacu mor* and tells us it was 'the marshy ground disputed in a lawsuit', although there is no record of such a case. Musberry Lane leads past 'the mouse burrow' and possibly somewhere infested by the rodents. However, it could be a derogatory name, as is Lush's Cottage and Lush's Farm, renamed sometime during the nineteenth century as it was considered indelicate to refer to somewhere as Maidenshole Farm — but the meaning is the same.

MARSHWOOD

Found in 1188 as Merswude, this comes from Old English *mersc wudu* and is 'the wood by a marsh'.

MARTINSTOWN

A name which has only been in existence since the fifteenth century, for the original place name was 'the stream often only flowing in winter'. Here the name is recorded as Wintreburne in 1086, as Wynterburn Seynt Martyn in 1280, and as Martyn towne in 1494. These records show how the basic name was stated as having a church dedicated to Saint Martin in the thirteenth century and which eventually dropped the original name entirely.

MELBURY ABBAS

A basic name which comes from Old English *maele burh*, 'the multi-coloured fortified place', and a general reference to the area, has the addition from Latin *abbatissa*, or 'abbess', from it once being held by Shaftesbury Abbey. The name is found as Meleburge in 956, Meleberie in 1086 and Melbury Abbatisse in 1291.

Local names include Budden's Farm, remembering Roberd Buddon who was here in 1564; the local pub is the Glyn Arms and recalls the former landholders; the coppice known as Pug's Parlour is a reference to the 'place occupied by the upper servants in a large house', hence was seen as unreachable or perhaps higher quality; and there can be no doubt as to the meaning of the winding road known as the Zigzag.

In 1853, a new building was erected; the building was to house the local policeman and his family, thus providing free accomodation for the local bobby. Although the building is no more the location is still known as Copper's Corner.

MELBURY BUBB

Another 'multi-coloured fortified place', this addition is first seen in 1244 as Melebir Bubbe and reminds us the Bubbe family were lords of this manor by 1244.

MELBURY OSMOND

Here the 'multi-coloured fortified place' is from it being held by a man called Osmund, as evidenced by the record as Melebury Osmund in 1283.

The locals and passing trade are extended a warm invitation, not only by the management and staff but by the very name of the Rest & Welcome Inn.

MELBURY SAMPFORD

Old English *maele-burh*, or 'the multi-coloured fortified place', is found as Melebury Sunford in 1312, a reminder this was held by the Saunford family from at least the thirteenth century.

MELCHOMBE REGIS

Seen in 1223 as Melecumb, this comes from Old English *meoluc cumb* and lterally describes 'the valley where milk is produced', i.e. a well-established and productive dairy farm. The addition is not for distinction, but shows 'royal approval'.

MELCOMBE HORSEY

A name found as Melcombe in 1151, Melecum in 1158, Melcumba in 1210, Milecumbe in 1229, and Melcombe Horsey in 1535. As with the previous name this is from Old English *meoluc cumb*, or 'the valley where milk is produced'. The addition, to distinguish it from the previous entry, is manorial with the Horsey family in possession from the sixteenth century. Prior to this, the place was held by the Turges family, and there are several records of the place name with the earlier name.

Minor names here include Bingham's Melcombe, a smaller manor that was held by the de Byngham family from 1243; Henning Hill describes itself as 'the high hill'; Dorsetshire Gap is a gap in the hills here where several tracks converge; Giant's Graves and Giant's Stones are traditionally held to be the missiles that two giants threw to one another during a battle, although they are glacial in origin.

MELPLASH

Here is a strange name that comes from Old English *maele plaesc* and describes 'the multi-coloured pool'. Now, clearly, water is a colourless liquid, and any colours present in the water itself would mix, thus the reference is either to the vegetation, the soil, or more likely both. The name is found in 1155 as Melpleys.

MILBORNE ST ANDREW

Records of this name include Muleburne in 934, Meleburne in 1086, and Muleburne St Andrew in 1294. Here is Old English *myln burna*, or 'the mill stream', with the addition from the dedication of the church.

Locally is Deverel Farm, originally a separate manor which still occupies the northern part of the parish. This name refers to the family who held this manor; the de Deverell family are recorded here from at least the fourteenth century. However, this place has only recently been known by this name, for many years it was Milborne Deverel, the now lost element clearly referring to the 'mill stream'. This is not the only lost name,

Hunter's Moon at Middlemarsh.

for until about the eighteenth century there was also a Milborne Mamford, Milborne Michelston and Milborne Symondeston.

MILBORNE STILEHAM

Listed as Meleburne in Domesday, as Myleburn Munketon in 1292, Mullbourne Beke in 1326, Little Mellburne in 1332, and Milborne Stylam in 1431, the basic name here comes from Old English *myln burna*, which simply means 'the mill stream'. The records of 1292 and 1326 show possession by the abbey of Bec-Hellouin, the record from 1332 shows this is the smaller settlement compared with the previous entry, while the current addition is from Old English *stigel hamm*, 'the place by the steep ascent'.

MILTON ABBAS

Milton is a very common place name and invariably from Old English *middel tun*, or 'the middle farmstead'. Many common names have a second element; here the second element comes from Latin *abbatis* and meaning 'of the abbot', and this shows this place was part of the property held by the local abbey. The name is recorded as Middeltone in 934, Mideltune in 1086, and Middelton Abbatis in 1268.

An old Minterne Parva farm building.

Minor names here include Chescombe Farm and Chescombe Lane, which stem from *cirice cumb* describing 'the church in the valley'; the name of Delcombe refers to 'the valley of the wood'; East Luccombe and West Luccombe share a name meaning 'the valley with a shelter' or perhaps should be understood 'the sheltered valley'; Barnes's Hill reminds us of the family of Nicholas Bern who were here by 1317; and Hoggen Down describes 'the hill of the young sheep'.

In 1742, the eldest daughter of the Sackville family, earls of Dorset, Lady Caroline, married Joseph Damer, 1st Earl of Dorchester. They moved into Milton Abbey ten years later after extensive refurbishment and, when his wife died in 1775, he named part of the fabulous estate Lady Caroline's Drive in her memory.

In the middle of the eighteenth century, the estate was sold to the Hambro family, who in turn sold it on in 1932. Today, the mansion is the excellent Milton Abbey School, an independent establishment with facilities most schools would envy. Two of the six boarding houses are called Damer and Hambro to remember the previous owners, while the local public house is the Hambro Arms.

MINTERNE MAGNA

With the earliest surviving record from 987 as Minterne, this name is thought to come from Old English *minte aern*, or 'the house near the place where mint grows'. The addition, which is compartively recent, is from the Latin magna meaning 'great'.

The church at Minterne Magna.

MORCOMBELAKE

Even though the earliest surviving record of this name comes from 1550 as Morecomblake, the name certainly pre-dates this by several centuries. It comes from Old English *mor cumb lacu* and describes the 'stream in the marshy valley'.

MORDEN

Domesday records this name as Mordune, which speaks of 'the hill in the marshland' and comes from Old English *mor dun*.

Local names include Sherford Farm, which stems from scir ford, or 'ford over the bright one'; Whitefield Farm is historically listed as Whitewell, from Old English *hwit wella*, or 'the white or bright stream'; Brookes Farm is a reminder of former tenant John Brookes, here in 1664 and in the same year William Coillins was living at Collins's Lane; Fry's Wood was associated with William le Frye in 1332 and, again, that year was also when Goodwin's Lane was home to Stephen Godwyn; The Hang is derived from an early Modern English word hang meaning 'slope, bend'; and Lousley Wood, from Old English *hlose leah*, comes from 'the woodland clearing with a pig sty'.

MORETON

Moreton is among the most common place names in England, and the surprise here is that there is no second defining element. Listed as Mortune in Domesday, here is 'the farmstead in marshy ground or moorland' and comes from Old English *mor tun*. While it might seem difficult to see moorland and marsh being in any way similar, both were represented by Old English *mor*, so it is sometimes difficult to see which was intended.

Other place names here include Hurst, a common element *hyrst* and seen all over England as 'the wooded hill'. The Broad is a reference to a particularly wide part of the river Frome; the Frampton Arms reminds us that the Frampton family held this manor from 1376; the Obelsik was erected in 1785 in the memory of James Frampton; and while Dick o' th' Banks may be interpreted as a sprite or an imp, it is simply a late Middle English variation of Richard Banks.

A glass or two can be enjoyed in the Frampton Arms, a name that commemorates the family who were living at the manor house since the fourteenth century. Even in the twentieth century the Framptons were still influential when they rented a cottage on Clouds Hill to Thomas Edward Lawrence, who was stationed at nearby Bovington. Lawrence of Arabia, as he is almost always known, died on these lanes, following a motorcycle accident at the age of forty-six, and he is buried in a simple grave in the church here. Conspiracy theory has even found its way to Moreton, and reports of a mysterious black car conflict with two boys on pushbikes.

MOSTERON

Recorded in Domesday as Mortestorne, this comes from a Saxon personal name and Old English *thorn* and describing 'the thorn tree of a man called Mort'.

Customers and landlords of the Admiral Hood have never been able to discern which of the famous naval family is honoured by the name of the pub. The best-known Hood was the battle cruiser that famously sank the German ship Bismarck in 1941. This was named from the family, which included Admiral Viscount Hood (1724-1816) who was a mentor to Horatio Nelson; his younger brother Alexander, Admiral Viscount Bridport (1726-1814), who fought in both the French Revolutionary and Napoleonic Wars; Vice-Admiral Sir Samuel Hood (1726-1814) whose ship Zealous played an important role in the Battle of the Nile; Admiral Lord Hood of Avalon (1825-1901) who fought in the Crimean War and later served as First Sea Lord; and Rear-Admiral Sir Horace Hood (1870-1916) whose vessel HMS Invincible was lost with him aboard at the Battle of Jutland.

MOTCOMBE

The earliest record of this name is as Motcumbe in 1244. Here is the Old English *mot cumb*, or 'the valley where meetings are held'. The moot or meeting in question would have been between local tribal representatives in the hope of working together for their mutual benefit.

Coppelridge derives its name from Old English *coppod ac hrycg* and describes 'the ridge at the pollarded oak tree', a name which almost paints its own image. The basic name of Enmore Green comes from 'the duck pool', and the addition is self-explanatory. Bittles Green was associated with the family of John Budel in 1397; Brickells Pond Farm must refer to the family name of John Brickell, here by 1627; Payne's Place was associated with William Payn in 1455; Pottle's Hill takes the name of fourteenth-century resident William Potel; Quoits Copse is a rather fanciful corruption of the name of William le Coyt, here by 1292; and the name of Bridewell Lane comes from the term for 'a prison', here used as a derogatory term for 'a remote and/or infertile plot of land'.

Cowherd Shute Farm is a reminder of John Couhirde, here by 1313, with *sceot* telling us there was a 'steep slope' nearby. Fishy Mead Copse has a small stream that would have been where fish were caught for the table.

Larkinglass Farm is recorded in the early nineteenth century as being named from a larking-glass, 'a machine with mirrors used to attract larks to the net'. However, all references to this 'machine' seem to have emanated from this one record and thus, unless this was a machine of local construction, may well have been the result of some unknown urban myth.

King's Court Palace sounds very grand indeed, but these three elements are not all as they are understood in the twenty-first century. The reference to the monarch is actually to the royal hunting lands hereabouts, the court refers to the royal retinue who were hunting, while the palace is a corruption of palis or paleis and tells of 'a fence of pales, a palisade'.

MUDEFORD

Even today it is possible to see this as 'the muddy ford', a warning that the river bottom was obscured and so to watch your step. The name comes from Middle English *mudde-ford*, and is not named from the River Mude itself, which comes from the place name, a process referred to as back-formation.

Chapter 13

Netherbury to Nottington

NETHERBURY

Recorded as Niderberie in 1086, Domesday's record shows this to be from Old English *neotherra burh* and describes this as 'the lower fortified place'.

NETTLECOMBE

Here is a name coming from Old English *netele cumb*, or 'the valley where nettles grow', and is listed as Netelcome in 1086.

NEWTON MAIDEN

Newton is a very common place name and, rather predictably, refers to the 'new farmstead' from Old English *niwe tun*. Such common names often have a second distinctive element. Here it is in the form of a Middle English addition telling us it was the place 'of the maidens', a name which probably identifies this as being held by nuns. The name is recorded as Neweton in 1086 and as Maydene Neweton in 1288.

NORTH WOOTTON

With several Woottons in Dorset, the addition is to be expected and is self-explanatory. This place is listed as Wootton in 1180, Wotton Episcopi in 1316, and not as Northe Wotton until 1569. This name is from Old English *wudu tun* and refers to 'the farm in or near a wood'. Note the fourteenth-century record from *episcopi* and referring to 'the bishops of Salisbury' who were in possession of the manor for many years.

Clotfurlong Lane tells of the 'clump of earth at the plough length' — the original meaning of furlong and not an exact measurement. Snagharbour Wood takes here *beaorg*, or 'shelter', and *snag*, which either means 'a tree stump' or is from Dorset dialect snag meaning 'sloe', the fruit of the juniper.

NOTTINGTON

Seen in 1212 as Notinton, here is a Saxon personal name with Old English *ing tun* and describing 'the farmstead associated with a man called Hnotta'.

Chapter 14

Oakley to Owermoigne

OAKLEY

A common place name and one recorded as Ocle in 1327. This is from Old English *ac leah* and a reference to 'the woodland clearing where oak trees are seen'.

OBORNE

Found as Womburnan in 975 and as Wocburne in 1086, this comes from Old English *woh burna* and refers to this being the '(place at) the crooked or winding stream'.

OKEFORD FITZPAINE

Domesday records this name as simply Acford in 1086, and not until 1321 do we see an addition as Ocford Fitz Payn. This basic name comes from Old English *ac ford*, 'the ford by the oak trees', with the addition a reference to this manor being held by the Fitz Payn family, who were certainly here by the thirteenth century.

Local names include Belchalwell, which was originally from *ceald wella*, or 'the cold spring', to which was added the name of Bell Hill or 'the bell-shaped hill'. Darknoll Farm is still easy to see as 'the dark hillock', Fiddleford Bridge was built where there was earlier a river crossing known as 'Fitela's ford', and Hile Farm and Hile Coppice both describe 'the nook of land'.

Lowbrook Farm is not what it seems but comes from a Saxon personal name and is 'Lulla or Lolla's brook'. Stroud Farm is derived from *strod*, a term describing 'the marshy land overgrown with brushwood'. Angers Farm can be traced back to Baldewyn Aunger, who was here by 1315. Early records of Banbury Hill point to this coming from *bana burh*, or 'the murderer's fortified place', presumably where the felon's remains were left hanging as a gruesome warning to others.

However, surely the best place name here is Room Farm, best seen as being used in the sense 'roomy' for it refers to a rather spacious house here. However, early records show the original name was a humorous one and based on Middle English *rum hous*, not exactly 'roomy' for this was a jocular reference to the large house as 'the privy'.

ORCHARD (EAST & WEST)

With less than a mile between the two, one is clearly an offshoot of the other. These names are seen as Archet in 939 and which is thought to come from Celtic *ar ced*, or 'the place at the wood'.

Hargrove Farm took its name from 'the woodland grove frequented by hares' (not harts); Fishey Lane is a corruption of *wisc ieg* and 'the dry land in the marshy meadow'; and Swainscombe Farm takes the name of 'the valley of the herdsman'.

OSMINGTON

Listed as Osmingtone in 934 and as Osmentone in 1086, this features a Saxon personal name and Old English *ing tun*, which tells us of 'the farmstead associated with a man called Osmund'.

Local names include Ringstead, from Old English *hring stede* and describes 'the place with a ring'. There is no ring visible here today, so we can only speculate on an enclosure, stone or some other circular feature. Upton was 'the higher farmstead', and Frenchman's Ledge is a coastal feature wthat took the name of Thomas le Freynsch, here in 1318 and quite likely of some French ancestry.

The local is the Sunray, a pub with a sign displaying a broadly smiling face on a sun, a rather different way of suggesting a warm welcome.

OWERMOIGNE

Even for southwestern England, this is a highly unusual place name indeed. The name is found as Ogre in Domesday and as Oure Moyngne in 1314 and features two elements. First is the Celtic *ogrodust*, a word referring to the gaps in the chalk hills here, which act as funnels for onshore winds. This is followed in the fourteenth century by the name of the lords of the manor; the Moigne family were known to have been here by the thirteenth century, and thus this name is the '(place at) the wind gaps of the Moigne family'.

Chilbury is the only surviving reminder of the old hundred (a Saxon administrative region) of Celberge, and the corruption is to be expected. Thus this is from Old English *cealc beorg* or 'the chalk hill'. Galton gets its name from *gafol tun*, the 'farm subject to a tax or rent', the payment most likely being made to the lord of the manor of Owermoigne.

Holworthy describes 'the enclosure in a hollow'; offshore rocks are named the Bear, the King and the Split Rock, only the last is obviously named for its appearance; and Burning Cliff, a reminder of the bituminous shales here which burst into flame in 1826, an example of spontaneous combustion that was to produce a fire which burned for four years.

Chapter 15

Pamphill to Puncknowle

PAMPHILL

A name not seen before 1168, when it is recorded as Pamphilla. This comes from one of two possible Old English origins, either this is *pamp-hyll*, quite literally 'hill, hill', or the first element is a personal name and thus 'Pampa or Pempa's hill'.

Local names include Abbott Street, Abbott Farm and Abbott Copse, all with a common origin showing possession by the abbey of Sherborne, with the Street being a Roman road to Poole Harbour. Barford Farm speaks of being 'the woodland grove near the ford', while Old Barford probably shares more than just a name, at one time were home to two halves of a single community; and Barnsley Farm began life as 'Beornheard's woodland clearing'.

Bradford Farm was near 'the broad ford'; Chilbridge is either 'Ceola's causeway through marshy ground' or the first element is *ceole*, 'throat, channel', and thus a narrow passage; Eye Meadow is from Middle English ile maed, or 'the island meadow'; Stone Farm was near 'the boundary stone'; Tatten is from *tadde haefen*, 'the haven for toads'; Fitche's Bridge refers to the Fitch family who lived at High Hall in the eighteenth century; Gillingham's Almshouses were founded by Roger Gillingham in 1695; Old Lawn Cottages and Old Lawn Farm were once referred to as 'old land', indicating this was abandoned arable land

PARKSTONE

The earliest surviving record of this name is dated 1326 and is exactly as the modern form. This is hardly surprising as the two Old English elements are little different from the two syllables. Old English *park* and *stan* combine to tell of 'the boundary stone of the park'.

North Haven Lake is still a sheltered part of the bay that gave it a name. Salterns Beacon and Salterns Pier mark where a property was used for the making or selling of salt, and there are innumerable references to salt production in this area over many years. Britannia Road takes its name from the former Britannia Inn, here by 1826. Bullpitt Beacon took the name of an offshore feature resembling a 'bull pit', the name coming from *bula pytt*. In 1543, Anna Weston's family gave their name to Weston's Island and Weston's Point.

Flag Head Chine and Flag Farm must refer to some feature thought to resemble the flower of a flag or iris. That this was where a flag was hoisted is unlikely, as this would have been common to many points around the natural harbour. It will hardly be a surprise to find that the names of Lilliput House and Lilliput Pier are related to the famous work *Gulliver's Travels* by Jonathan Swift. One Isaac Gulliver was living at Lilliput House, so named by 1783, and there is a record of a baptism of the Gulliver family in 1823 when a boy was named Lemuel, the same name as the hero in Swift's novel. As the book was first published in 1726 there can be no suggestion that the characters were based on these people, clearly the reverse was the case. However, it is unclear if the original Mr Gulliver in Parkstone was born into a family of that name, or if their name was changed to fit the apparent fantasy.

The local here is the Grasshopper; the image on the sign does show a large green insect, so there cannot be any other reason for this name.

PENTRIDGE

Recorded in Domeday as Pentric in 1086, it was earlier found in a document dating from 762 in exactly the same form. This comes from two Celtic words *penn* and *tyrch* and refers to this as 'the hill of the boar'.

Buckley comes from *bucc leah*, or 'the woodland clearing where male deer are seen'; Chettle Head comes from *ceotol* meaning literally 'kettle' and describing the shape of the 'deep valley surrounded by hills'; Grim's Ditch is most likely a by-name of the pagan god Woden, here associated with the earthwork; while Morgan's Lane is named after the family of William Morgan, here by 1548.

PIDDLE (RIVER)

An Old English river name which, when used as a noun, is derived from *pidele* and refers to 'the marsh or fenland', although perhaps as this is applied to the river it should be seen as that which is draining off from this area.

PIDDLEHINTON

Found in Domesday as Pidele, the addition is not seen before 1244 as Pidel Hineton. These two elements together tell a lot about this place as being 'the farmstead on the River Piddle worked or owned by a religious community'. Here the river name comes from Old English *pidele*, 'the marsh or fenland', with the addition from *hiwan-tun*.

Bourne Farm is easy to see as being named from *burna*, Old English for 'stream'. However, good researchers always check everything, even the blindingly obvious, and old records of this name suggest that while this has always been the name of the farm, the stream itself was known differently. Today, the stream has no name, it is but a minor tributary of the River Piddle, yet in the past seems to have been referred to as Burnstow, the second element here is stow, which has several similar meanings depending upon the usage. Here it is probably suggesting 'an assembly', but any important meeting place or court can be ruled out. Without written evidence, we need to look for clues elsewhere to discover what any assembly was seeking. There is but one resource here, water, and we can only conclude this was being used for bathing or perhaps washing of clothes or, and this seems more likely, a regular watering place for cattle.

Other names here include Muston Farm, and the family of de Musters were here from 1303. Heave Coppice, Heave Farm and Heave Rookery share an origin from heave meaning 'a heap, hillock', the name also being transferred to several fields.

Local pubs here include the Thimble, a thatched inn with the River Piddle running through the grounds. The reason for the name is a mystery, it does not seem likely that the place took the name because of an alternative trade of the landlord, the most likely reason is of a collection of thimbles once housed here. The earliest known thimbles are found in Roman settlements, but the first thimbles found in England date from 1695 and were made from a Dutchman named Lofting. However, he is not the reason for the modern name of the European, the second pub in the village, which was named to show that the United Kingdom is now a member of the European Common Market, now the European Union.

PIDDLETRENTHIDE

As with the previous name, this place takes the name of the River Piddle 'the marsh or fenland'. However, here the addition is from Old French *trente* and Old English *hid*, giving 'the farmstead on the River Piddle of thirty hides'. A hide was an area of land that is thought to have averaged roughly 30 acres. This name is recorded as Uppidelen in 966, Pidrie in 1086, and Pidele Trentehydes in 1212.

PILSDON

Domesday records this name as Pilesdone, which comes from Old English *pil-dun* and describes this as either 'the hill with a peak' or 'the hill marked by a stake'.

PIMPERNE

Found in a document of 935 as Pimpern and in Domesday as Pinpre, this is either from Celtic *pimp-prenn* meaning 'the place among the hills' or the first element is Old English *pimp* and thus 'the hill called Prenn'.

Other names here include Nutford Farm and Little Nutford, both names from 'the ford where nuts grow', this crossing the River Stour; Cowards Farm was worked by Nicholas Coward in 1664; Letton is from *leac tun*, or 'farmstead where herbs are grown'; Poor Delf was 'the poor's pit'; and Prior's Lane reminds us these lands were held by the priory of Breamore in Hampshire.

PLUSH

From Old English *plysc* and recorded as Plyssch in 891, this name refers to the '(place at) the shallow pool'.

The King Charles public house, Poole.

POOLE

Listed as Pole in 1183, this name comes from Old English *pol* and refers to this as the '(place at) the pool or creek'.

Street names of the famous port include Bay Hog Lane, probably a personal name describing 'a hunter of hogs'; Drake Street, and formerly Drake Alley, are named after a woman called Frances Drake who was living here in 1697; similarly Skinner Street was associated with Skinner Alley, both reminding us of John Skynner and Grace Skyner, seventeenth-century inhabitants, but the name may have applied to the tradesman for years prior to that.

Other local names include Hospital Island, from the old isolation hospital; Church refers to that once dedicated to St James; Baiter refers to the 'projecting strip of land'; and Back Water Channel points to this as being mooring off the main channel.

Several pubs in the famous old port remind us of the links to the sea, including the Cockleshell, the Jolly Sailor, and the Lord Nelson (the man who has more pubs in England named after him than any other individual). Tradesmen are marked by the Bricklayers Arms and Foundry Arms, and the Spotted Cow may have been named to encourage farm workers but is more likely to have been an easily recognised image. However, the Sweet Home Inn is certainly an invitation to find a home from home within.

The Lord Wimborne is named for Viscount Wimborne of Canford Magna, the peerage created in 1918 for Ivor Guest. The Shah of Persia was named to mark the visit of the shah to England and to Poole in 1887. However, the best name here is the Dorset Knob, a dry savoury biscuit of crumbly consistency, which is the traditional accompaniment of Blue Vinny, the famous cheese of Dorset.

POORTON (NORTH & SOUTH)

Found in Domesday as Pourtone, here is a name thought to be an old and unknown river name with Old English *tun* or 'farmstead'.

PORTESHAM

Records of this name begin with Porteshamme in 1024 and exactly as the modern form in Domesday. Here is Old English *port hamm*, referring to 'the hemmed in place of the town', the town thought to be Abbotsbury.

PORTLAND BILL

A name not seen before 1649, although it must surely have been in existence well before this, it comes from Old English *bile*, literally 'a bill, beak' and referring to the shape of the promontory here.

POWERSTOCK

Domesday records this name as Povrestoch, showing this is identical to the first element of Poorton and an unknown and lost river name preceding Old English *stoc* or 'outlying farmstead'.

POXWELL

Records begin with Poceswylle in 987 and as Pocheswelle in 1086, this Old English name comes from either a Saxon personal name with Old English *swelle* and 'Poc's steeply rising ground' or the suffix may be *wella* and thus 'Poc's spring or stream'.

Field names here include Butt Meadow, the butt here being the strip of unploughed land where the plough team turned; Hoopers Cottage was home to John Hooper in 1332; Voxcombe Meadow is a corruption of 'fox valley'; and Waryhall Bottom and Waryhall Hill have a common origin in *wearg halh* and meaning 'the nook of land of the felon or felons'.

POYNINGTON

From a Saxon personal name with Old English *ing tun* and referring to 'the farmstead associated with a man called Punt', the only record of note dates from 1086 as Ponditone.

PRESTON

This is a common place name and one which comes from Old English *preost-tun* and refers to 'the farmstead of the priest'.

Local names include Plaisters Lane, recorded as Playstrete in 1465 and showing this was where regular games or sports were held. Verlands Road is from an old field name furlang, which describes the distance that could be ploughed by a team before they required a rest and equated to the standard imperial distance of 220 yards or one furlong.

Chalbury takes the name of 'the encampment of the peasants'; Lodmoor describes 'the track across the marsh'; Rimbrow Coppice stands at 'the barrow or hill on the border'; Boiling Rock was the site of a bubbling spring; Roman Bridge was not built by the Romans but the villa nearby was; and Winslow accurately refers to a 'small round hill'.

The local pub was once known as the Old Ship, a reference to the link with the sea and possibly through a former landlord or owner. Since it was refurbished it has been renamed the Spice Ship, which alludes to a connection with the days when this was the most valuable commodity and the huge values coming through the East India Company. However, there is no proof that this place ever had any connection with the spice trade.

PUDDLETOWN

Another name derived from the River Piddle. Here the name speaks of 'the farmstead on the River Piddle', where the Old English *pidele* speaks of the river running through the 'marsh or fen'. The name is records as Pitrestone in 1086 and as Pideleton in 1212.

The origins of the lost settlement of Bardolfeston is still seen in the surviving names of Bardolf Manor, Basan Hill and Basal Plantation, albeit the last two have been corrupted through local pronunciation. These places took the name of the Bardolf family — and Ralph Bardolf was here by 1244 — who descended from Bardulf de Chiselburneford, another lost settlement named from the stream which gave rise to Cheselbourne. Druce Farm is also named from a member of this family, and Drogo Bardolf is mentioned in a record of Bardolfeston dated 1242.

Other names include Duddle Farm, either from Middle English *dodde*, 'the hill', or from a word derived from this, the early Modern English *duddle*, 'teat, nipple', in which case describing the shape of the hill. Ilsington began as 'the farmstead associated with a man called Aelfsige'; Waterston House took the name of 'Walter's farmstead'; Yellowham Hill is from *geolu hamm*, or 'the yellow hemmed in land', the colour referring to this being sandy soil; Chine Hill is from *cinu hyll*, the 'hill with or by a ravine'; Kite Hill is the place where these birds were seen; Martins River Island is named from the Martin family who had land here from the fourteenth century; from Old English *hraefn beorg*, or 'the barrow frequented by ravens', has evolved the name of Rainbarrows; and Troy Town Copse remembers a maze of that name in 1839.

The local is the Blue Vinny, a pub named from the Dorset cheese, which was especially popular in the nineteenth century. A mature cheese, it gets its name from the blue veins running through it.

PULHAM

A name recorded in Domesday as Poleham, here is a place name from Old English *pol* or *pull* with *ham* or *hamm*, and thus this is the 'homestead or hemmed in land by the pools'.

The name of Cannings Court has an interesting history. It began as Canons in 1212, a name which alludes to it being a possession of Cirencester Abbey. Quite coincidentally, the name then changes to reflect it being the home of the family of Thomas Canon. This gentleman is first named in 1327 in a document that also cites him as the highest taxpayer in the parish. Lipgate Farm was the site of a 'leap gate for deer', the name coming from Old English *hlip geat* and referring to a fence low enough to be cleared by deer but containing the livestock that grazed there.

At Pulham we find the Halsey Arms, a pub that can only have been named after the family who were created Baronet Halsey in the nineteenth century. It is difficult to be certain which member of the family was the inspiration for the name, but perhaps it was the 3rd Baron, Thomas Halsey, who served as captain in the Royal Navy from 1916 until 1946. He also managed to find time to play cricket for Cambridge University, the Royal Navy, and Hertfordshire as a batsman and fast bowler.

PUNCKNOWLE

Domesday gives this place names as Pomacanole, thought to come from a Saxon personal name with *cnoll* and describing 'Puma's hillock'.

Chapter 16

Radipole to Ryne Intrinseca

RADIPOLE

Found in Domesday as Retpole, this name can still be seen as coming from Old English *hreod-pol* and describes the '(place at) the reedy pool'.

Buckland Ripers is another of those place names that come from Old English *boc land* or 'the land granted by charter'. Here the addition refers to the family of John de Riuers who held this manor by the thirteenth century and who came from Riviere in Normandy. Tatton Farm is derived from 'Tata's farmstead', and Loscombe refers to 'the pig sty in the valley'.

RAMPISHAM

The earliest surviving record comes from Domesday as Ramesham. Names ending in -ham are often difficult to define for there are two very similar elements, which are often impossible to separate. Old English *ham* is quite simply a 'homestead', but the almost identical *hamm* is probably best described as 'hemmed-in place'. A *hamm* should not be seen as a fortification but a natural barrier on at least two and probably three sides. Such barriers may not be seen today for they could simply have been vegetation or a marshy land that was drained long ago.

In the case of Rampisham, however, it is not the suffix which is uncertain but the first element, for here the suffix is certainly Old English *hamm*. The first element has three alternative Old English elements: *hramsa*, a term referring to 'wild garlic' and the one which seems the most likely; *ramm*, a 'male sheep'; or Ramm, a personal name.

RYNE INTRINSECA

At first glance this seems to be a complex name. However, the earliest record is from 1160 when the name appears simply as Rima, itself clearly Old English *rima* and the '(place at) the rim, edge, border'. Much later the affix appeared, a Latin term meaning 'inner' and to distinguish it from the now lost manor of Ryme Extrinseca or 'outer'.

Chapter 17

St Ives to Symondsbury

ST IVES

A name also seen in Cornwall and Cambridgeshire, places that are much better known and have influenced the development of this name, for St Ives has no religious etymology. Recorded in 1167 as Iuez, this comes from Old English *ifet* and describes this settlement as being 'overgrown with ivy'. The additional 'Saint' did not appear until comparatively recently, seemingly a deliberate move to associate this place with the other places but for reasons unknown.

SANDBANKS

A name not seen before the beginning of the nineteenth century, Sandbanks is self-explanatory.

SANDFORD ORCAS

Recorded in Domeday as Sanford in 1086 and as Sandford Horscoys in 1372. Here is a common name, coming from Old English *sand ford* and quite obviously the '(place at) the sandy ford'. To distinguish this from other Sandfords there is a second element, here from the Orescuils family who were lords of this manor from at least the twelfth century.

   The name of Hail seems to have lost its second and final syllable, for originally this appears to have been from *heg leah*, which would have been expected to become Hayley, or 'the woodland clearing where hay is cut'. Penmore Road is named after the land known as *peo mere*, 'the pool where gnats or similar insects proliferate'. Weathergrove Farm takes its name from 'Wedera's woodland grove'; Benchy Hill is located near 'the enclosure on the shelf of land'; and the name of Jerrards reminds us that Johannes Gerard was here in 1464.

SEABOROUGH

Found in Domesday as Seveberge in 1086, this name comes from Old English *seofon-beorg* telling us it was the '(place of) seven mounds or barrows'.

The image of old Shaftesbury welcomes present-day travellers to the town.

SHAFTESBURY

A name listed in 877 as Sceaftesburi and in 1086 Sceftesberie, this comes from Old English and is either *sceaft burh*, 'the fortified place on a shaft-shaped hill', or the first element might be a Saxon personal name and thus 'Sceaft's fortified place'.

Street names here include Bell Street, named from the Bell Inn and earlier referred to as Lawrence Street from the Church of St Lawrence. Bleke Street is a corruption of the family of Walter le Blyck who was reeve of the town in 1314. Christy's Lane remembers the Christie family, owners of Belmont House in the nineteenth century. Haimes Lane is named after John Haymes, who had a tenement here in 1348. Stoney Path, which is self-explanatory, was formerly known as Laundry Lane and was where the linen of the convent was washed in the well at the bottom of the slope. There was a tanner working in Tanyard Lane, as shown on the map of 1615. The name of Tout Hill is an old name for the 'look out hill' from *tot hyll*. Victoria Street was named to commemorate the diamond jubilee of Queen Victoria in 1897.

Alcester is transferred from the place name in Warwickshire meaning 'the Roman stronghold on the River Alne', and the abbey held lands here from at least the thirteenth century. Holyrood Farm also refers to this abbey in being the place of 'the holy cross'. Barton Hill Farm refers to 'the barley farm or outlying grange', a common name

Mustons Lane, Shaftesbury, after the seventeenth-century landholder, William Muston.

showing this was an outlying area used in the growing season to produce corn for the community. Layton House takes the name of another specialised farmstead with the name telling it us was 'the herb garden' from Old English *leac tun*.

The famous advert for Hovis featuring the young boy pushing his bike up the cobbled street was made here in Shaftesbury. Laden with loaves of bread and with a broad Yorkshire accent voicing over the images, there can be few who recognise these images are almost as far away from the Yorkshire Moors as it is possible to get.

SHAPWICK

Domesday records this name exactly as it is seen today, this shows the name comes from Old English *sceap wic* and describes this as 'the farm specialising in the rearing of sheep'.

Local names include Badbury Clump and Badbury Rings, an Iron Age hillfort, which is recorded as Vindocladia during the Romano-British period. This refers to 'the town with the white ditches', a reference to the white chalk soil found here. The modern name of the place describes 'the fortified place of a man called Badda', this being a Saxon personal name which shows it cannot have been known by this name prior to the arrival of the Saxons in the fifth century.

Horsecastles Lane, Sherborne.

White Mill shows it was stone built, hence the reference to it being 'white' rather than wooden. Bishop's Farm shows this manor was held by the archbishop of Canterbury and the bishops of Winchester and Durham over the centuries; and Piccadilly Lane was jokingly likened to the famous London street.

Crab Farm is undoubtedly the most interesting name here, for this is said to be where the accursed Shapwick Monster was seen. 12 October 1706, and a fishmonger is wheeling his cart past this place. At the time he was not aware that a large live crab had fallen from the cart and he continued on his way. The villagers of Shapwick spotted the creature and, having never seen the like of it before, were very much afraid. When one of the older members of the village declared it a 'monster' they attempted to defend themselves with sticks and other assorted impromptu weapons.

As the group fought their 'ferocious battle' with the monster, the fishmonger returned having discovered the loss of the crab, which would earn him a good price. Intrigued by the commotion, he approached and smiled as he took in the scene. Calmly, and to the astonishment of the Shapwick villagers, he lifted the large crustacean and placed it in his basket before continuing on his journey ensuring he tell anyone who would listen of the incident he had just witnessed at Shapwick.

Since that time, the villagers of Shapwick dare not reveal the name of their home to any fishmonger for fear of ridicule. However, one resident can laugh at themselves, for at Crab Farm the weathervane shows the villagers bravely facing the fearsome Shapwick Monster.

An ornate roadsign at Horsecastles
Lane, Sherborne.

SHERBORNE

A common place name often found with an addition for distinction. Here the name
comes from Old English *scir burna*, or the '(place at or by) the clear or bright stream'.
Listings of this name include Scireburnan in 864 and as Scireburne in 1086.

Street names here include Acreman Street, from *acer mann* or 'farmer, ploughman'
and where such lived and/or worked; Bristol Road was once the main road to that city;
Cheap Street is from *ceap* meaning 'market'; Factory Lane was the road to Westbury
Silk Mills; Priestlands was a part of the land given by Bishop Joselin for the building of
St Thomas's Chapel; and Tinneys Lane was named after the family of Henry Teny, here
by 1476.

Ludbourne Road preserves the name of 'the dirty brook'; Clanfield is taken from
the field name meaning *claene feld*, or 'the open land cleared of weeds'; and while
Trendle Street clearly refers to a *trendel* or 'circle, ring', that feature has long since been
eradicated from the landscape. George Street took the name of the George Inn, which
once stood here; while Half Moon Street is named after Half Moon Cottage, itself
formerly the Halfmoon public house.

Quarr Lane features a dialect word for a 'quarry'. Digby Road takes the name of the
well-known and important family who lived near here. Coldharbour normally refers to
'a shelter from the cold', but there is evidence to suggest this may be from Old French
col d'arbres and thus describing 'a clump of trees'. Ottery Lane is named after the Ottery

family who were here by 1290, and Tinneys Lane remembers a John Tinney who lived here during the reign of Elizabeth I.

Hyle Farm was located at 'the nook or corner of land'; Lenthay Common was 'grazed only in Spring' — that is, around the Christian period of Lent. Westbridge Farm stands at the place where the road from the south crosses the River Yeo, but is west of the town. Pageant Gardens were named after the pageant of 1905 as part of the town's celebrations commemorating 1,200 years since the founding of the abbey.

Public houses in Sherborne include the Mitre Inn, the name of the pointed hat worn by bishops, although here the association with the abbey. The Fountain most often is heraldic, showing an association with the Plumbers' Company or the Master Mariners.

The Tippling Philosopher recalls a former customer who is claimed to have walked the 300 yards to the pub and staggered the same distance home. Described as a natural philosopher, Robert Boyle (1627-91) is best known as a scientist. Indeed, as any school pupil will know, he formulated what became known as Boyle's Law, which relates to the volume, pressures, and temperature of gases.

SHILLINGSTONE

This name is found as Shillyngeston in 1444, a name referring to it being 'the *tun* or farmstead of Schelin'. Oddly there is an earlier record in Domesday, which includes the name of the tenant at that time, the great census listing this place as Akeford Skelling.

While Alder's Coppice is clearly the '(place at) the alder trees', this place has been known by other names, including 'alder way', 'the place below the alder trees', 'the place above the alder trees', and a thirteenth-century alternative of 'Aelfric's river meadow'. Bere Marsh Cottages, Bere Marsh Farm, and Bere Marsh Mill share the origin of Old English *baer mersc* and describe 'the woodland pasture by the marsh', while Bonsley is from 'Buna's sheep pasture'.

SHIPTON GORGE

Listed as Sepetone in 1086 and as Shipton Groges in 1594, this name comes from Old English *sceap tun*, or 'the farmstead where sheep are raised'. The addition, necessary when the place name is as simple and common as this, refers to the lords of the manor the de Gorges family, who were certainly here by the thirteenth century.

SILTON

A small parish and one that, as with so many others, has its earliest surviving record dating from 1086 and the Domesday survey as Seltone. Later records include Selleton in 1230, Salton in 1268, Cylton in 1327, and as the modern form by 1332. Together these records seem to point to Old English *sealh tun* and describe 'the farmstead near the willow copse'.

Local names include Feltham Farm, a name from 'the hemmed in land where hay was cut'; Card's Farm gets its name from the family of John Card, here by 1664; Slait Barn is from *slaeget* and stands at 'the sheep pasture'; and Wyndham's Oak recalls Sir Hugh Windham who came here from Somerset shortly after 1660 and bought the manor of Silton.

SIXPENNY HANDLEY

Records of this name are found as Hanlee in 877, as Hanlege in 1086, and Sexpennyhanley in 1575 with the basic name coming from Old English *heah leah* 'the high woodland clearing'. The addition here is an old hundred name, a hundred being an administrative sub-division of a county and said to be sufficient to sustain approximately one hundred households. Such divisions were first seen in the seventh century and remained until the nineteenth century. The name itself comes from Old English *Seaxe* and Celtic *penn*, 'the hill of the Saxons'. As the name of the hundred this was recorded as Sixpenny Handley.

Local names include Bugden Bottom, describing 'the valley of the beech trees'; the suffix *denu*, or 'valley', is also seen in the name of Dean Farm; Frogmore Farm is named from 'the pool frequented by frogs'; Gussage St Andrew refers to 'the rushing stream' with the dedication of the church for distinction; Minchington Farm was a possession of the Bendictine nunnery of Shaftesbury, hence the name meaning 'the farmstead associated with the nuns'; Mistleberry Wood is derived from *micel burh*, or 'the big fortified place'; and a smaller earthwork is named Church Barrow from St Andrew's church.

Bridmore Ride is a track through the woodland, which is derived from 'the bridle path'; Drow Coppice is from a dialect drock describing 'a flat stone across a ditch, a covered well'; Endless Pit is not a literal name but describes a very deep pit; Humby's Stock Coppice is named after the family who owned lands here in the nineteenth century; Pollards Wood most likely refers to 'pollarded trees'; from 'the valley where privet grows' comes the name of Pribdean; and Five Ways is now the name given to a point where six tracks meet. There are also the dual names of Inward Lardenhall and Outward Lardenhall, two coppices either side of Oxford Street, which seem to be facetious eighteenth-century names for 'the lords' hall'.

SOUTHBOURNE

A modern creation, named to compliment the other suburbs of Northbourne and Westbourne in Bournemouth.

SOUTH PERROTT

This name appears as Pedret in 1086 and as Suthperet in 1268. This is undoubtedly from the name of the River Parrett, although this is an obscure name that has never been explained.

Here the local pub is the Coach & Horses, a name that invariably indicates this was a coaching inn, almost a 'bus stop' of the coaching era.

SPETISBURY

A name not seen before 1068, when it is recorded as Spehtesberie, this features a description and produces an instant snapshot of the area in Saxon times. Here the name comes from Old English *speoht-burh* and refers to 'the earthwork frequented by the green woodpecker'.

Local names include Clapcott's Farm, a place associated with John Clapcott in the early nineteenth century, and St Monica's Priory, which was occupied by various communities of nuns between 1800 and 1927.

The pub here is the Drax Arms, named after the family who built the estate with the huge arched gates alongside the A31, topped by a massive deer and a lion, which cannot fail to catch the eye of those who pass in their many vehicles each and every day. The Drax family can trace their power back to Henry Drax who, in 1680, was reported to be the one of the two most powerful businessmen in Barbados, sending sugar worth in excess of £5,000 each and every year.

Of course, this wealth and power owed virtually everything to the workforce, and the workers had been shipped here forcibly, courtesy of the slave trade. The Drax family were one of several Dorset families who made their money courtesy of the slave trade, some of whom were brought back to work as servants on their estates. While the families certainly exploited the workforce, it should be noted they were also some of the most vociferous in campaigning against the continued use of slavery.

STALBRIDGE

Records of this name begin with Stapulbreicge in 998 and Staplebrige in 1086, showing this comes from Old English *stapol-brycg* and referring to the 'bridge built on posts or piles'.

Here we find Antioch Farm, and the name refers to this manor being held by the family of Roger de Antioche who were here by 1244. Frith Farm comes from Old English fyrthe meaning 'woodland', the name also seen in Frith House and Frith Wood. Pile Lane and Pile Coppice are derived from *pil* and refer to a 'shaft, stake' and would have marked an area or boundary. Gummershay Farm features an Old German personal name and speaks of 'Gummer's enclosure'.

Stalbridge Weston clearly takes its name from the parish, the addition showing it was situated west of the main settlement. Basel Bridge probably takes the surname Basil or perhaps Bazell; Cook's Lane is named after former resident Thomas Cooke, who was here in 1664; Gray's Farm was home to Roger Grey in 1332; Hewlatt's Farm was associated with Mary Hulett in 1664; Landshire Lane lies on the county boundary as the name suggests; Shipney Lane was the site of the *scypen*, or 'cow shed'; and Waterloo Lane was doubtless named following the news coming through of the decisive victory against Napoleon at the battle of that name in 1815.

STANTON ST GABRIEL

The basic name here comes from Old English *stan tun* and describes 'the stony farmstead'. Listed as simply Stantone in Domesday, the addition refers to the local church. The settlement lies on the western slope of Golden Cap which, at 618 feet, is the highest cliff on this part of the south coast of England. The village fell into decline with the promise of work in Bridport, and erosion of the main road moved it inland, making the village virtually isolated.

STEEPLE

Recorded in Domeday as Stiple, this name has nothing to do with a church but comes from Old English *stepel* and refers to 'the steep place'.

Minor place names of this parish include Blackmanston, which is derived from 'Blaecmann's tun or farmstead'. Gaulter is from gold hord, which can still be seen as indicating where a 'golden hoard, a treasure' was once found although no record of such has ever been traced. Lutton refers to 'Lutta's farmstead'; Drinking Barrow refers to a tumulus alongside a ditch; Hurst Mill derives its name from miller Henry Hurst, here in 1636; and Old Bond Street is named after the local Bond family, while alluding to the much grander London street of this name.

The most interesting place name here is Hurpston, which, although it has proven difficult to define with any certainty, has led to some interesting speculation. The least likely today would be Old English *hearpere*, which would refer to 'the river occasionally dried up', for it has never been known to run dry in living memory. If the beginnings are understood as Old French *la harpin* then this could be 'the murmuring brook'. However, the most delightful is the local tradition that this refers to the large stone to the west of the place. Rising some nine feet above the surroundings, it appears to lie against the grain of the local rocks. Furthermore, it is said that the grooves on the surface can create a harp-like tone when the wind blows across them from the right direction.

STEEPLETON IWERNE

Found in Domesday as simply Werne, in 1210 as Steepletone, and the earliest surviving record of the two names together is from 1346 as Iwernestapleton. Although some sources suggest an origin from an unknown river goddess, this is probably 'the yew tree river' following 'the farmstead with a church or steeple or tower'.

Ashy Coppice remarks on the number of 'ash trees'; Beckford Lodges takes the name of the Beckford family, here in the eighteenth century; Everly Hill Farm is from *eofor leah*, or 'the woodland clearing where wild boar are seen'; Smugglers Lane is self-explanatory, while Grammars Hill is from a family name.

STINSFORD

Found in Domesday as Stincteford, this name is derived from Old English *stint ford* and tells us of 'the ford frequented by the sandpiper or sunlin'.

Here we find Bhompston Farm and Bhompston Cottages, which share an unusual name referring to 'Boneville's tun of farmstead on the River Frome'. Lower and Higher

Bockhampton describe 'the farm of the Bochaeme', the tribal name referring to 'the dwellers by the beech tree'. Coker's Frome Farm is named after John Coker, who was here by 1433, and Frome Whitfield was home to William de Whitfield's family early in the thirteenth century.

Drong is a rarely used word, but always used to describe 'a narrow way between hedgerows'. Similarly, the name of Snail Creep is applied to a narrow plantation — its narrow passage jokingly described as being so small that only a snail could get through it. Headless William's Pond is near the stone called Headless William, thus telling that this old stone cross long ago lost its top. Melstock began as a fictional place. Based on Stinsford, Melstock was the birthplace of Thomas Hardy and renamed for his novels.

STOBOROUGH

As with the previous name, the earliest record of this name is from Domesday. Listed in the great tome as Stanberge, this name is derived from Old English *stan beorg*, or the '(place at) the stony hill or barrow'.

STOCKWOOD

Listed as Stocwode in 1221, this name refers to 'the secondary settlement of or by the wood'. The name is also recorded as Stokes sancti Edwoldi in 1238, this referring to 'the outlying settlement associated with the church or chapel of St Edward'.

STOKE ABBOTT

Here is a *stoc*, or 'outlying settlement', which is associated with the abbey, presumably that at nearby Beaminster.

STOKE WAKE

There are records of Stoche in 1086 and Stok in Blakemore in 1285, which is the same year as the present form is seen for the first time. Old English *stoc* is one of the most common place names in England and refers to 'the outlying or secondary settlement'. The addition is manorial, referring to the family of Ralph Wake who were here by 1285. The other reference in that same year is the name of the forest on 'the black moorland'.

Whitecombe's early records do not clarify if this comes from 'the white valley', from Old English hwit cumb, or from *wid cumb* and 'the wide valley'. Balmers is a name seen several times, all coming from the family of John Bambflet who were here from 1332; Kate's Copse points to the tenancy of Mistress Kete, here in 1640; another tenant by the name of Mr Ridout gave his name to Ridouts Farm.

STOUR (EAST & WEST)

Domesday recorded this name as Sture in 1086, a name that is taken from the River Stour, which is also known as the Hampshire Stour. This is a Celtic river name meaning 'the strong one'. The additions are for two places well under a mile apart and are self-explanatory.

Local names at East Stour include Black Venn, a name speaking of 'the dark-coloured fen'. Peter Bullien's family were at Bullen's Farm by 1572; Cole Lane and Cole Street Farm most likely point to 'where charcoal was carried'; Hunger Hill is from *hungor*, a derogatory name for poor ground and which was also applied to Hunger Coppice and Hunger Farm; Lintern Lane is probably 'where flax or lint was available' and stems from Middle English *lynnet*; Pennymoor Pit Farm can only be an allusion to a penny rent; and Witch Lane is not the meeting place for the local coven but is derived from *wice geat*, 'the gate by the wych elm'.

At West Stour we find the Lynch telling of its location at the 'ridge', and Church Farm is associated with the church of St Mary's, itself built on a chapel always recorded as called the Hermit.

STOURPAINE

Found in Domesday as Sture and as Stures Paen in 1243, as with the previous entry, this name is taken from the Hampshire Stour. Here the river name meaning 'the strong one' is joined by the Payn family, lords of the manor from at least the thirteenth century.

Other names found in this parish include Ash Farm, predictably found near 'the ash trees'; France Farm, allegedly representing a family name, although the owner's nationality is a more plausible argument; Hod Hill, 'the hill with a shelter'; and Paradise Pond, which was considered most pleasing on the eye. Yet the most interesting name is that of Lazerton Farm, most likely from Old English *laecere* and describing 'the gatherer of leeches', doubtless plentiful in parts of the Iwerne.

STOUR PROVOST

A third entry named from the Hampshire Stour, a river name referring to 'the strong one', this name is recorded as Stur in 1086 and as Sture Preauus in 1270, the addition referring to this manor being held by the Norman Abbey of Preaux during the twelfth and thirteenth centuries.

Locally we find Duncliffe Hill, a name from *dun clif*, or 'the steep slope or bank of the hill'. Shade House Farm comes from a natural feature called a sceard and meaning 'a cleft, a gap (in a fence, hedge, etc)'. Terrace Farm is something of a misnomer, for it comes from a surname and the family of William Terry, here by the early fourteenth century. Wadmill Farm is derived from 'Wada's hill'; Butts Lane ran along the ploughed land with 'short strips at right angles to others'; Chequer Farm is probably known for its 'land of chequered appearance'; Good's Farm was home to the family of William Good in 1664; Hawker's Lane remembers Robert Hawker, here by the late seventeenth century; and Yeatman's Farm was worked by the family of Richard Yateman who were here by 1664.

STOURTON CAUNDLE

As discussed under Caundle, this element has never been understood. The addition comes from the river name meaning 'the strong one' with Old English *tun* or 'farmstead'.

Local names here include Bilcombe Copse, which comes from 'Billa's *cumb* or valley'; Brunsell's Farm is 'Brun's hill', a name shared by the hundred; the Jubilee Oak was planted in 1897, marking the diamond jubilee of Queen Victoria; Cockhill Farm is from *cocc hyll*, or 'the hillock hill'; Woodrow Farm is marked by 'the narrow row of trees'; and Cat Lane was formerly Catherine Wheel Lane, itself taking the name of the Katherine Wheel public house, which was later changed to the Trooper Inn, a name which referred to the volunteer army members, principally those who were to defend the nation against the very real threat of invasion by the French under Napoleon Bonaparte.

STRATTON

Odd to find this name without an addition, for it is found several times across the southern counties of England, each time with a distinctive second element. The name comes from Old English *straet tun* and describes 'the farmstead on the Roman road'.

Local names include Grimstone or 'Grim's farmstead', featuring an Old Norse personal name; Langford Farm is 'the long ford' across Sydlign Water, a tributary of the Frome; Wrackleford Coppice gets its name from Wraecwulf's ford'; the Coronation Plantation commemorates the official crowing of Edward VII; and Kidney Plantation is named from its shape.

The names of Great War Plantation and Prisoners of War Plantation were named for the large POW Camp three miles distant at Dorchester, which held Germans in 1915-16.

STUDLAND

Found in Domesday as Stollant, this name comes from Old English *stod-land* and speaks of 'the cultivated land where a herd of horses are kept'.

Claywell gets its name from Old English *claeg wella*, 'the clay spring or stream'; Handfast Point is from *han faesten*, 'the high stronghold'; Salterne first appears in the fifteenth century and marks the place where 'salt was made or sold'; and Newtown is as it seems, the 'new farmstead', a planned settlement laid out in 1286 complete with houses, streets, a market, a church, and a harbour.

The name of Agglestone refers to a large block of ironstone, some 20 feet thick and over 80 feet around. Known locally as the Devil's Nightcap, it is said to have been cast from the Isle of Wight by the Devil in order to demolish Corfe Castle, but it landed short. The official name comes either from Old English *halif stan*, 'the holy stone', or *hagol stan*, 'the hailstone'. Off the headland stands Old Harry, the largest of two sea stacks of chalk and likely another reference to the Devil.

STURMINSTER MARSHALL

Records of this name begin with Sture Minster in the ninth century, Sturminstre in Domesday, and as Sturministre Marescal in 1268. Here the Hampshire Stour, a river name meaning 'the strong one', combines with Old English *mynster* or 'large church' with the additional reference to the Mareschal family who were lords of this manor from the thirteenth century.

Ball's Lane is named after William Ball, recorded here in 1627; East Almer Farm gets its name from 'the eastern eel pool', a valuable commodity in medieval England; while Bailie Gate, Bailie House and Bailey Gate Station are from Old English *baillie*, describing 'a bailliff's district' and possibly indicating this officer's place of work. Henbury Farm tells us it was at 'the high or chief place'; Moorcourt Farm shows the location of the 'manor house'; what was 'the western woodland clearing' is now known as Westley Farm; Austen's Plantation was associated with Thomas Asten in 1664; Crumpets Farm and Lower Crumpets share an origin of crumb pytt telling of 'the crooked pit'; and Notting Hill is probably transferred by someone from the place in London made internationally famous by the film of that name.

STURMINSTER NEWTON

Records of this name include Nywetone at Stoure in 968, Newentone in 1086, and Sturminstr Nyweton in 1291. Sturminster Newton was originally two places on opposite banks of the Hampshire Stour. As with the previous entry, the one place takes its name from 'the large church on the river called Stour'. The second place is derived from Old English *niwe tun*, or 'the new farmstead'.

Gough Close was named after the family of John Goff who was here by 1511, with Thomas Goffe here by 1664, the same year as William Penny's family were living in Penny Street. In 1839, the Ricketts family were living in what is now Rickett's Lane, and Market Street speaks for itself.

Bagber is derived from 'Bacca's woodland grove'; Colber Crib House was built on the land known as 'Cola's woodland grove'; Coombs is a name referring to 'the valley; the old royal demsne on the hill is today marked as Kingsdown; Perry Farm was located 'at the pear tree'; and Piddles Wood is not a river name but either a personal name as 'Pyttel's enclosure' or perhaps stems from *pyttel worth*, 'the hawk's enclosure'.

The 'farmstead for growing rye' is today known as Rixon; Dunch Mouth is from *dyncge mutha*, 'the well manured land near the confluence of the rivers (Divelish and Stour)'; Hewlett's Drove is the way used by herdsmen and which was associated with the Hulett family by 1664 when Dinah Hulett was recorded here; Honeymead Lane ran alongside 'the sweet meadow or pasture'; and Queen's Coppice is a reminder that part of this manor was granted to Queen Katharine in 1544.

Road Lane is a most interesting name, and it is a lane and not a road. The name is derived from Old English *atte rod*, or 'at the clearing', and is associated with Robert de la Rode and William atte Rode who were here by the early fourteenth century.

One pub here is the Green Man, a name invariably linked with Robin Hood and his Merrie Men in the modern era. While the character of Robin Hood may be questioned, there can be little doubt these men wore green attire, either the famous Lincoln green or more likely the darker Kendal green. However, these were no outlaws but foresters and woodsmen.

SUTTON WALDRON

A name found in 932 as Suttune, in 1086 as Sudtone, in 1212 as Suttone, and as Suttone Walerand by 1297. Here is a name that is found throughout England and still easy to see as 'the southern farmstead'. The addition is from Waleran, who was 'the huntsman' and tennant-in-chief at the time of the Domesday survey, while his descendants were still here by 1210 in the shape of Walter Walerand.

Satan's Square is a local name referring to the earthwork marked as 'The Devil's Trencher and Spoon' on a map dating from about 1765.

SWANAGE

Listings of this name include Swanawic in the late ninth century and Swanwic in Domesday. From Old English *swan wic*, this is either 'the farm of the herdsmen' or 'the farm where swans are reared'.

Street names here include Battle Mead, taken from a meadow of this name where the Saxons and Danes fought; Bondfields Avenue, which is associated with the family of William de Boneuile, here by 1288; Eldon Terrace was named from Earl Eldon who held land here; Howard Road likely took the name of the family of Elizabeth Howard who was certainly here in 1664. Isle of Wight Road cannot lead to the island but does allow views from the cliff; however, Lighthouse Road does lead to the lighthouse. Sentry Road led to an old watchtower or observation post, and Townesend Road is from Old English *toun ende*, literally the end of the town at that time.

Burnhams Lane takes it name from Tom Burnham's Oak, a tree which, according to local tradition, was named after a man buried beneath its branches — those who commited suicide were not permitted to be interred in consecrated ground. Manor Road took the name of the manor house that was here, but it changed its name to the Victoria in 1835 after the then Princess Victoria stayed here.

Around this area we find minor names such as Godlingston Farm, which was once a settlement known as 'Godelin's farmstead'; what was 'the farmstead associated with a man called Here' is now seen as Herston; Moulham describes 'Mula's homestead'; Ulwell Farm and Ulwell House both refer to a 'spring or stream frequented by owls'; Anvil Point is said to have had a rock resembling an anvil; while Giant's Grave and Giant's Trencher are names given to two low tumuli.

Caldron Barn Farm is a corruption of *cawel* and has nothing to do with witches but refers to 'farm or barn of the cabbages'. California Farm does not share the crops of western USA, but is named such as a remoteness name, a humorous comment on a distant corner of the parish. Conner Cove is a sea cave, likely named from cunner and/or conner, names given to two fishes of the wrasse family, which would have preferred the rocky bottom here.

There is also the name of Half Moon, a slight cove that has been suggested as being named for its shape. However, this slight indentation is more crescent moon and has led

Swanage town sign.

to the tradition that this stretch of the coast was navigable assuming the light was as bright as that of a half moon, and thus Half Moon is a name attributed to smugglers.

The ancient stone quarry known as Tilly Whim Caves has two elements of interest. There are records of this family name dating back to Roger Tilie in 1332, although this is not to suggest that this was the family who were mining, The second element comes from *whim* or 'windlass', thus where the stone was lowered down to the waiting boats.

Public houses in Swanage include the Black Swan Inn, a pub name with a long history, which dates back to at least the sixteenth century. However, the reference is Roman in *rara avis*, or 'rare bird', for black swans were unknown until the discovery of Australia in 1770. Thus the reference as an early pub name is thought to describe another rare bird in a special landlord. The Crows Nest Inn is clearly a maritime reference; the Globe Inn is a popular name and an easily recognisable image; and the Village Inn conjures up the a very welcoming, quintessentially English rural scene, even when the pub is in the middle of a major city.

SWYRE

From Old English *sweora* and describing the '(place at) the neck of land', the place is listed as Suere in Domesday.

SYDLING ST NICHOLAS

Found in 934 as Sidelyng and as Sidelince in 1086, this name comes from Old English *sid hlinc*, or 'the broad ridge'. Here the addition is taken from the dedication of the church.

SYMONDSBURY

A place name derived from a Saxon personal name and Old English *beorg*, here is 'the hill or barrow of a man called Sigemund'. Domesday lists the place as Simondesberge.

Chapter 18

Tarrant to Tyneham

TARRANT, RIVER

A river name which is probably from an old Celtic term referring to the river literally as 'the trespasser' and a name describing it as most likely to flood. The name has formed the basis for several place names.

TARRANT CRAWFORD

Recorded as Tarente in Domesday and as Little Craweford in 1280, this takes its first element from the River Tarrant defined under its own listing. Here the second element is from Old English *crawe ford* and meaning 'the ford frequented by crows'. As can be seen there was a brief period during the thirteenth century when the name of the river was not used for this settlement, this was simply Little Crawford.

Here we find Ellen's Coppice, which can only be referring to Queen Eleanor, while Tarrant Abbey Farm remembers the abbey dedicated to St Mary & All Saints.

TARRANT GUNVILLE

As with the previous name, this place is listed in Domesday as Tarente, representing the River Tarrant, which is discussed under its own heading. By 1233, the name appears as Tarente Gundevill, the affix reminding us that this manor was held by the Gundeville family from at least the twelfth century.

The name of Bussey Stool is seen three times here, this coming from the family of John Busse, here in 1664, and from stol, which refers to 'tree stumps'. Stubhampton is from Old English describing 'the farm of the dwellers by the tree stump village'. Bloody Shard Gate is traditionally the site of numerous battles by the keepers on Cranbourne Chase and those who were regularly poaching the deer, the name also influencing Blood Way Coppice, which historically was the self-explanatory name of 'flood way'. Harbin's Park is one of several names that refer to the family in possession of this estate in the eighteenth century. Loose Path Coppice refers to 'the path to the pig sty'; Rowden Coppice is from *ruh den*, or 'the rough hill'; Windmill Plantation refers to the site of an old windmill marked on the map of 1618; and Zareba Clump is derived from the Arabic *zariba*, or 'fenced enclosure or camp in the Sudan', which must have been brought back to this country during the British colonial period.

TARRANT HINTON

Featuring the name of the River Tarrant, defined under its own listing, this name is recorded as Terente in the ninth century, as Tarente in Domesday, and as Tarente Hyneton in 1280. This addition is from Old English *hiwan-tun*, 'the farmstead of the religious community'. It should not be thought to have been where religious figures lived and worked but a region that belonged to the church and, in this case, Shaftesbury Abbey.

Hyde Farm takes its name from *hid* or hide, a measurement of land capable of supporting a family; Barton Hill takes its name from 'the barley farm' here; and Ninety Eight Plantation and Ninety Nine plantation can only have been planted in the years of 1898 and 1899 respectively.

TARRANT KEYNESTON

Another place name taking the name of the River Tarrant, or 'trespasser', discussed above. This name appears in Domesday as Tarente and in a document of 1225 as Tarente Kahaines. The addition is from 'the farmstead of the Cahaignes family', lords of this manor from the twelfth century.

Ashley Wood is a corrupted name for the road, itself taken from the wood as seen in Old English *aesc leah weg*, or 'the way by the woodland clearing near the ash trees'. Buzbury Rings is a difficult name to define but could represent 'the ring ditches of Beorhtsige's fortified enclosure'.

The local here is the True Lovers Knot, showing an image of the double-loops in which are often represented images of the bride and groom. Today only seen in imagery, formerly they were made and could be worn in the hair when made of silk over a more rigid frame.

TARRANT LAUNCESTON

Recorded in Domesday as Tarente and in 1280 as Tarente Loueweniston, the addition referring to 'the *tun* or farmstead of a man called Leofwine or the family known as Lowin'. The name of the River Tarrant is discussed under its own entry.

Old Butts is a name given to the old archery butts, Penfold Belt reminds us of a time when stray animals were rounded up and held here by the pinner until collected by their own and released on payment of a fine, and Race Down reminds us that Blandford races were held here in July or August from the eighteenth century.

TARRANT MONKTON

This place on the River Tarrant, see above, is recorded as Tarente in Domesday and as Tarent Moneketon in 1280. Here the addition comes from Old English *munuc tun*, or 'the farmstead belonging to the monks', specifically those who were attached to Tewkesbury Abbey.

Local names include Luton Farm meaning 'the farmstead of a man called Lufa'; Old Butts refers to the former archery targets; and Turner's Lane was home to John Turner in 1664.

TARRANT RAWSTON

Found in Domesday as Tarente in 1086, this takes the name of the River Tarrant. Much later the name is recorded as Tarrant Rawston alias Antyocke in 1535, where the addition tells us it was then 'held by a man named Ralph' and had earlier been the domain of the Antioch family.

TARRANT RUSHTON

The last of the places named after the River Tarrant, which appears as Tarente in 1086 and as Tarente Russeus in 1280. Here is a name that shows the manor was 'the farmstead or *tun* held by the Rusceaus family' who are recorded as having been here in the thirteenth century.

Preston Farm is listed as a separate manor in Domesday, later found as Tarrant Preston (1545) and Preston Parva (1559). This basic name is quite common, referring to 'the farmstead of the priests', and thus an addition to distinguish this place from other Prestons is to be expected. These additions refer to the river and from the Latin *parva*, or 'little'. Abbeycroft Coppice and Abbeycroft Down are further evidence of this being held by the church.

Bratch Coppice and Bratch Lane are derived from *braec* describing 'land broken up for cultivation'; Chalcott's Coppice refer to 'the cold cottages'; Harry's Coppice is a reminder that the family of William Harris were here by 1664; Hogstock Coppice comes from 'the outlying farmstead for hogs'; and Smith's Cottages were built on 'the land of John the smith'.

TALBOT VILLAGE

A very recent name for a very recent place, Talbot village was built as a model village in the decade of the 1860s. The place was named in honour of the two Talbot sisters who had held land here.

THORNCOMBE

One of two Dorset places of this name, this one is near Blandford and is recorded as Tornecombe in Domesday. This name comes from Old English *thorn-cumb* and describes 'the valley of the thorn trees'.

THORNCOMBE

This place is found as Tornecoma in 1086, a village near Holditch, which is another 'balley where thorn trees grow'.

THORNFORD

A name listed in 951 as Thornford and in 1086 as Torneford. This name comes from Old English *thorn ford*, or 'the ford where the thorn trees grow'.

Boot Lane is named after the Boot Inn, here from 1849. Gaul Hill overlooks the field with 'the barren or wet spot', from Old English *gealla*, and is where two streams meet. From *weg furland*, or 'the furlong of land beside the road', comes the name of the house known as Waverlawns.

TINCLETON

A name found in Domesday in 1086 as Tincladene, which can be seen as coming from Old English *tynincel denu*, or 'the valley of the small farms'.

Local names include Napier's Close, a reminder that this was once home to the family of Nathaniel Napier, and the wonderfully named Skating Pond, which needs no explanation but instantly paints an idyllic rural winter scene to rival any festive greetings card.

TODBER

Listed as Todeberie in 1086, this name features a Saxon personal name followed by either *beorg* or *bearu* and describing 'Tota's hill' or 'Tota's grove'.

Red Lane takes its name from the colour of the sandstone around here, and it is also the name of a tiny hamlet and gave its name to a hundred, which is remarkable for such a small place and was possibly chosen as a neutral venue. Hunt's Hill and Gannetts are undoubtedly from family names, although there is no surviving record of either family here. Shave Lane was also seen in the names of Great Shave, North Shave and Cathshave — self-explanatory additions to Old English *sceaga*, or 'small wood'.

TOLLER (FRATUM & PORCORUM)

Records of this quite unusual name include Tolre in 1086, while the additions first appear in 1350 as Tolre Fratum and Tolre Porcorum. The basic name is that of the river, today known as the Hooke but formerly called the River Toller. This is an old Celtic name meaning 'the hollow stream'.

The additions are clearly of Latin derivation, yet are as unrelated as any two additions could be. The addition of Fratum or 'of the brethren' refers to possession by the Knights Hospitallers, while the Latin Porcorum means 'of the pigs' refers to a place where herds of swine were a permanent feature.

Tuckton bridge.

TOLPUDDLE

Domesday records this name as Pidele, which by 1210 was listed as Tollepidele. Here is 'the farmstead on the River Piddle of a woman named Tola'. The river name, which is discussed under its own entry, follows the name of a Scandinavian woman who is known to have donated her lands here to the church at Abbotsbury Abbey some time before 1066.

Locals enjoy their favourite tipple in the Martyrs Inn, recalling the group of farm workers who formed a trade union in the nineteenth century. Of the six all but one were released; James Hammett eventually returned to Tolpuddle and died in 1891 at Dorchester Workhouse. Recently, Hammett Close has been cut for a new housing development and named to remember the best known of the Tolpuddle Martyrs.

The name of Lovelace's Meadow is a reminder of the family of that name, the earliest record of which dates from 1664 when a certain Robert Lovelace was here. Years later, descendants of this family included James Lovelace and his brother George Lovelace, George's brother-in-law Thomas Standfield and Thomas' son John Standfield — all of whom were charged and transported along with Hammett.

TRENT

A place name originally applied to the stream here, Trent stems from a Celtic term meaning 'the trespasser' — warning it is liable to flood. The place is recorded in Domesday as Trente.

Here is Adber Farm, a name found as early as AD 956, and which was 'Eata's woodland grove'. Flamberts reminds us that Daniel Flmabert was here in the late eighteenth century. Hummer Bridge is named after a small tributary of the Yeo, which flows south of here. It is a British river name of uncertain meaning and origin and also seen in the better-known Humber.

TURNERS PUDDLE

A name that can only be found in England, it is recorded in 1086 as Pidele and in 1268 as Tonerespydele. As with other names, this takes the name of the River Piddle, discussed under its own entry, and includes the name of the Toner family who were lords of this manor from 1086.

Local names include Snelling Copse, Snelling Dairy, and Snelling Farm, all three sharing a common origin of a Middle English surname Snelling, which would have come from a Saxon personal name and thus referring to 'Snell's place'. Brockhill Coppice was riddled by 'badger holes'; Damerhill Coppice and Damerhill Cottages come from Old English *domere hyll* and meaning 'judge hill', which probably points to a meeting place, a court.

TURNWORTH

Recorded as Torneworde in 1086, this name comes from Old English *thyrne worth* and refers to 'the thorn bush enclosure'.

Local names include Brockham, which comes from brocc hamm, 'the enclosed area frequented by badgers'. Suggestions that this first element is from *broc* are highly unlikely for there is no brook in this valley, but it is possible there was a stream some time in the past. Derived from Old English *hring mere*, the name of Ringmoor speaks of 'the pool by the circular enclosure', this is the earthwork to the north of Turnworth. The Clapper Plantation takes its name from the clapper, or 'rough bridge'. Ewern Down Plantation speaks of 'the hill where ewes are grazed'.

TYNEHAM

A name that probably comes from Old English *tige-hamm* and describes 'the hemmed-in place where goats are seen'. The name is found as Tigeham in Domesday.

Minor names here include Baltington, or 'the farmstead associated with a man called Bealdheard'; North Egliston and South Egliston undoubtedly started as a single settlement described as 'Eggelin's farmstead'; Povington refers to 'the farmstead associated with a man called Peofa'; Worbarrow is probably 'the enclosure of the hill'; Earl's Kitchen refers to 'land granted to the Earl of Hertford'; Maiden's Grave Gate almost certainly refers to this as being where a woman was buried after she took her own life; and The Cat undoubtedly refers to a former inn of that name here.

Chapter 19

Upton to Verwood

UPTON

A common place name and one which comes from Old English *upp-tun* and, rather predictably, describes 'the higher farmstead'. The name is found as the modern form in 1463, and the only surprise here is that there is no second distinguishing element.

UPWEY

Records of this name include Waie in 1086 and as Uppeweie in 1241. Here is a name from Old English *upp* and the river name Wey, which is discussed under its own entry, thus 'the higher settlement on the River Wey'.

Local names include Elwell, which is from *haele wella*, 'the healthy spring', or possibly *haelu wella*, 'the healing spring'. Other names include Stottingway, meaning 'farmstead at the place cleared of stumps'; and the Windsbatch more likely 'the winding path of the hillock' than 'the windy hillock'.

VERWOOD

Verwood may have been the original name and the current name, but the Normans had another name for it. In 1288, this name is called Beuboys, from Old French *beu-bois* describing 'the beautiful wood'. The original is Old English and is recorded as Fairwod in 1329, which comes from *faeger wudu* and also means 'the beautiful (or fair) wood'.

The name of Ebblake Bridge comes from Old English *lacu* following a Saxon personal name and telling us of 'Abba's small stream', which marks the county boundary. Potterne Farm is first recorded in the late thirteenth century, when it was 'the building where pots were made' and presumably had been since before the Norman Conquest.

Baker's Farm was home to the family of John le Bakere in 1283. Budgen's Copse comes from Old English *bucc maed*, telling us of 'the meadow frequented by bucks or stags'. Crab Orchard was where 'crab apples grow'. Mount Ararat is named after the hill where Noah's ark is said to have come to rest following the Biblical flood and is not a mountain but is a prominent and remote hill of the parish.

Three Legged Cross is an interesting name with two equally plausible origins. For some this is a marker for a crossroads where three lanes met, and yet no map shows three lanes around the time when the name is first recorded. Other sources suggest this may have been the site of the gallows, which was nicknamed the three-legged mare from the seventeenth century.

Pubs here include the Albion Inn, an alternative name for England which probably comes from the Latin *albus*, or 'white', and referring to the first thing seen having cross the English Channel, the white cliffs of chalk. The Swans, being plural, is not heraldic but refers to the birds.

The Monmouth Ash is a pub name that is derived from one of the most significant times in Verwood's history. In 1685, the Duke of Monmouth was captured on Horton Heath following the massacre at the Battle of Sedgemoor. Monmouth had landed at Lyme Regis with eighty men, marching north to Somerset, and others joined his band of supporters to his claim to the throne. On 6 July 1685, the men were met by the forces of James II, led by John Churchill, who was later created Duke of Marlborough and was a direct ancestor or prime minister Sir Winston Churchill. Defeated, Monmouth fled back to Dorset with four colleagues — they were aiming to reach Poole and sail to Holland. The four split up and Monmouth disguised himself as a shepherd but was seen by Amy Farrant, an old woman who reported the information. A search revealed what looked like a pile of old clothes in a ditch, but turned out to be the eldest illegitimate son of Charles II, identified by the badge his father had given him.

Monmouth was dragged away to Ringwood and eventually put on trial at Dorchester in front of the infamous Judge Jeffreys and the Bloody Assizes. Monmouth was executed by beheading on 15 July of that year. The location beneath the ash tree became known as Monmouth's Ash, hence the name of the pub.

Chapter 20

Walditch to Yetminster

WALDITCH

A name found in Domesday as Waldic, this comes from Old English *wolu dic* and describes 'the ditch with a wall or embankment'.

WAREHAM

Records of this name include Werham in the late ninth century and Warham in Domesday. This is probably from Old English *waer-hamm* and describes 'the water meadow of or by the weir'. However, the second element here could have been Old English *ham* and thus 'the homestead by the weir'.

Streets of Wareham include Brixeys Lane, named after John Brixey who was here by 1747; Conniger Lane ran alongside a meadow of that name, describing 'the rabbit warren'; Shatter's Hill takes a family name, although whether this is Lawrence Shatter in 1664 or Walter Hatter in 1434; Howard's Lane is a corruption of Hayward's Lane, this the name of an officer of the borough in 1623, whose duties included keeping a watchful eye on the way the common land was used; and Roper's Lane, the lane where the ropemakers lived and worked.

Local names include Bestwall, which comes from Old English *bi eastan wall*, or 'the place by the eastern wall (of the town)'. The Fishery, this on the River Frome, is given as Elizabeth de Burgo's free fishery in 1327; East Holton and West Holton share a common origin of 'the farmstead in the hollow'. Eight Hatch Plant refers to floodgates or sluices on the river, presumably there were eight of them. Gore Fields comes from *gara*, an Old English word describing this triangular piece of land formed by the boundaries of the early roads.

Bloody Bank is so called from 1774 and was probably known as such, albeit unofficially, not long after 1684 when several men were tried, condemned and executed here, having been found guilty by the court of the infamous Judge Jefferies at Dorchester. Among them were a Mr Baxter and a Mr Holman, these men having supported the rebellion by the Duke of Monmouth. Nundico is an interesting place name, found twice around Wareham. It seems it must be from Latin *non dico* meaning 'I do not say', which is understood as being something or somewhere people were reluctant to talk about, or maybe it is simply suggesting the place had no name.

Shag Looe is a channel named from Shag Rock, this being an old name for the cormorant. Trigon House takes the name of Trigon Farm or Trigon Hill, from Middle English *trigon* or 'triangle' and describing the shape of either farm of hill. Wood Bar Looe is a channel that, at least at some point, was obstructed by a wooden bar. Woodbine Cottage would have had honeysuckle growing on or around it, and Youngs Farm was home to John Young in 1606.

A milepost outside Wareham.

Wareham town sign.

The pubs of Wareham include the Duke of Wellington, named after Arthur Wellesley (1769-1852) who became a national hero for leading the final defeat of Napoleon at Waterloo in 1815, the culmination of a distinguished military career. He later turned to politics, serving as prime minister (1828-30) and as foreign secretary (1834-35). His name is as popular today, and indeed there are more pubs named after this man than anyone but Lord Nelson.

The Weld Arms is named after the family who bought Lulworth Castle in 1641 through Humphrey Weld and is still owned by his descendants. The Horse & Groom is a reminder of when stabling was as commonly found in public houses as guest rooms. The Cock & Bottle is an advertisement for the product: the bottle is one method of serving ale and the cock was the name given to the spigot or peg which was used to draw beer from a barrel.

The Silent Woman is a pub name that is said to have been derived from the wife of an innkeeper. The premises were the secret meeting place for smugglers, but their secret was hardly likely to remain such owing to her wagging tongue in the market. The smugglers threatened to remove her tongue unless she held it.

WARMWELL

A name that virtually explains itself. From Old English *wearm-wella*, or 'the warm stream or spring', this name appears in the Domesday record as Warmewelle.

Locally we find Evening Ford, which cannot refer to the time of day but probably refers to a family who lived here, although there are no records to support this. Pole Coppice stands next to the 'pool' which gave it the name; Pats Castle Cottages is another unusual name, probably a jocular reference to someone who bragged about his home; Vyse Barn seems to take the name of Harry Vye, while earlier it was 'the stone enclosure'; Mynty Close describes 'the water meadow where mint grows'; and Rack Close and Tucking Mill Road are both references to cloth making, the place where the cloth was stretched out on a frame to dry.

WATERCOMBE

A name found in Domesday as Watrecome and in 1165 as Watercumbe. This comes from Old English *waeter cumb* and describes 'the wet valley'.

Bugs Lane comes from an old inhabitant in Saxon days, most likely the personal name Bug or Bugg, and the Walter Bukke who was here in 1332 took his name from the place. Blackland's Close was cut at the 'dark land'; and Chalk Pit and Gravel Pit are names that are self-explanatory.

WEST MOORS

Found as La More in 1310 and Moures in 1407, this name comes from the Old English *mor* meaning 'marshy grounds'. The addition here is self-explanatory.

WEST PARLEY

Domesday gives this name as Perlai, a name from Old English *peru leah* and describing the 'woodland clearing where pears grow'.

Dudsbury and Duds Bury are two places but share a common origin in 'Dudd's fortified place'; Bramble's Farm remembers the family of James Bramble, here in 1777; Dowager's Copse has no link to a grieving widow, this is simply a corruption of the family name of Walter Douge, who were here by 1327; Egypt is a remote corner of the parish, and the name rather exaggerates this; Gullivers Farm is nothing to do with the literary character created by Jonathan Swift but refers to former resident Isaac Gulliver, who was certainly here 1745-1822; Mag's Barrow refers to 'the tumulus of the Maggs family'; and Woolslope Farm is from Old English *wylla slaep*, or 'the muddy stream'.

The name of Dudsbury, discussed above, is also seen in the name of the pub. The Owl's Nest takes the image of the owl, even the word is synonymous with the night, and combines it with its home, thus suggesting that those abroad at night could find home from home here.

WEST STAFFORD

Listed in Domesday as Stanford in 1086, the name coming from Old English *stan-ford* and referring to the '(place at) the stony ford'. The addition is to distinguish this from other Staffords.

The minor place name of Frome Billet takes the name of the River Frome and adds the family name of William Belet, who was here by 1086, as detailed in Domesday. Conquer Barrow is a tumulus near to the Neolithic henge monument known as Mount Pleasant, and while the latter is a compliment to the productive soils here, the former seems to be completely arbitrary. Sixpenny Gate must refer to a toll or rent that was payable at the entrance point.

WEY (RIVER)

A British river name recorded as Waye in 1244 and Weye in 1367. Whilst the Celtic or British language is unrecorded, we can understand this tongue by comparison with the closely related languages of Welsh, Cornish and Breton. Thus this is most likely from something akin to Welsh *gwy* meaning 'the white or sparkling river'.

WEYMOUTH

A name referring to the '(place at) the mouth of the River Wey', the river name is discussed under its own entry. The second element here is Old English *mutha*, the place name first seen in 934 as Waimouthe.

Street names in Weymouth include Boot Hill, named from the Boot Inn. Great George Street is named from the visit of George III who visited Melcombe in 1789. The Duke of

Gloucester had a house in what is now Gloucester Row. Lydwell Close takes the name of 'the noisy stream'. St Albans Street reminds us the Duke of St Albans had a house in Melcombe Regis in the eighteenth century.

Melcombe Regis comes from Old English *meoluc cumb* and literally describes 'the valley which produces good milk', suggesting it is fertile. In the fifteenth century, the additional Rex indicates this is an ancient royal demesne, and it is now seen as Regis, which marks the visit by George III. Sluice Gardens marks where the sluice gate from Sutton was located on the road to Wareham.

The Mixen is an offshore ledge, which is from Old English *mixen*, or 'dung heap', thus suggesting was where the town dump was located. Indeed there is a record from 1620 stating that the dung heap in the Channel was washed away by storms and rain and ended up in the port. Thereafter, other measures were taken to solve this problem, although they rubbish was now being dumped on land.

Pubs here are named for Weymouth's close proximity to the sea. The Cutter Hotel remembers the single-masted sailing vessel known for its speed and manoeuvrability, which helped the excise officers in their pursuit of smugglers. The Admiral Hardy remembers Sir Thomas Masterman Hardy, 1st Baronet and who was alongside Lord Nelson when he was shot and mortally wounded. He is best remembered for 'Kiss me, Hardy' although, while often quoted as being such, these were not Nelson's last words.

The Marquis of Granby is a fairly common pub name, all named because of John Manners (1721-70). Colonel of the Royal Regiment of Horse Guards by 1758 and commander-in-chief of the British Army eight years later, the man's courage and leadership made him one of the most popular and inspirational leaders in British military history. The name was conferred on the large number of taverns their former commanding officer set up for so many of his men when they retired from the service.

The John Gregory is named after John Gregory Baldwin, late husband of Hilda Baldwin who officially opened the pub on 1 August 1980. It is a part of the Southill shopping centre, which was planned by Mr Baldwin, who sadly collapsed and died the previous year when development was still in its infancy.

The Duke of Albany was a title conferred on the fourth, and youngest, son of Queen Victoria, Prince Leopold, when he married in 1881. Born 7 April 1853, he died ten days before his thirty-first birthday, leaving a daughter, Princess Alice, Countess of Athlone, and his wife Princess Helena of Waldeck and Pyrmont, who was pregnant with the next his successor, Charles Edward, Duke of Saxe-Coburg and Gotha. He was one of the royals of Europe who had haemophilia, and when he was in Cannes — the warm weather was hoped to ease the pain in his joints, a common sympton of the haemophilia — he slipped and fell at the yacht club, injuring his knee. He died in the early hours of the morning, a rapid end hastened by the combination of morphine and the claret with which he had washed down his sumptuous evening meal.

WHATCOMBE

The earliest record found is as Watecumbe in 1288. Here is a name from Old English *waet-cumb*, 'the wet valley', or *hwaete-cumb*, 'the valley where wheat is grown'.

Wimborne Minster, town sign.

WHITCHURCH CANONICORUM

Records of this name include Witcerce in 1086 and Whitchurch Canonicorum as early as 1262. The basic name is a common one, from Old English *hwit-cirice* and describing 'the white church' and thus built from stone and not wood. The addition is Latin meaning 'of the canons' and a reference to possession by the canons of Salisbury. Interestingly, the church is dedicated to St Candida, an alternative name for St Wite and which is probably derived from the place name.

WHITCOMBE

Records of Widecombe in 843, Widicumbe in 1212, and Witcombe in 1460 show this to come from Old English *wid cumb*, or 'the wide valley'.

Locally is found the name of Culliford possibly referring to *cylfweard*, an Old English term describing 'the keeper of the mace' and one who presided over the court of the hundred. This is given added weight by this being the name of the hundred, officially termed Culliford Tree.

The thatched Coach & Horses, Wimborne Minster.

WIMBORNE MINSTER

A name found as Winburnan in the late ninth century, as Winburne in Domesday and as Wymburneminstre in 1236. Here is the first of two places that have taken the name of the local river, which stems from Old English *winn burna*, or 'the meadow stream', although the Wimbourne is today known as the River Allen. The addition here is from Old English *mynster*, or 'monastery, church'.

Streets here tell their own history. Cooks Row was where the cooks of Wimbourne sold their creations; Hanham Road remembers the family who were associated with this place; Legg Lane ran alongside 'the long meadow'; Market Way marks the road to the cattle market; Priors Walk was named to commemorate the birthplace of poet Matthew Prior (1664-1721); Redcotts Road and Redcotts Lane were named after the family of Maud Rotecod, who were here in 1327; Puddle Street would have had an almost permanent pool of muddy, even stagnant, water; while Pillory Street marks the site of this particular form of punishment, as did the former name of le Cokelymstole, or 'cucking stool'.

Other names here include Dean's Court, which was once home to the dean of the College of Wimborne Minster. Walford Bridge was built, as the name suggests, at the site of the earlier ford, one named from Old English *wealt ford*, which is literally 'the shaky ford' and points to one which is difficult to cross. Knobcrook is a district that gets its name from *knob*, or 'knoll', and *croc*, or 'bend', in a river or lane.

The Fisherman's Arms, Winkton.

The Willett Arms gets its name from land belonging to Ralph Willett from the eighteenth century. The Olive Branch is the universal symbol of peace, making it an ideal pub name. It is derived from the olive leaf brought back by the dove to Noah in Genesis, this scene is depicted on the arms of the Shipwright's Company, which is the likely route bringing the name to the pub.

WIMBOURNE ST GILES

As with the previous entry, this place takes the former name of the River Allen; from Old English *winn burna*, the Wimbourne speaks of 'the meadow stream'. This name is recorded as Winburne in 1086 and Vpwymburn Sancti Egidij in 1268, and Upwymbourne St Giles in 1399 (this addition refers to the dedication of the church).

All Hallows Farm is clearly taken from the dedication of the church, but this is dedicated to St Giles today and records confirm our suspicions of a change somewhere around the seventeenth century. French's Farm is officially named from the family of Richard le Franc, but clearly this surname indicates they had arrived here from across the English Channel.

Monkton Up Wimborne tells us this was 'the farmstead of the monks', which could be found upstream along the River Wimbourne. Oakley Down and Oakley Farm were named from 'the woodland clearing among the oak trees'. Sutton Farm and Sutton Hill

Thatched cottages at West Knighton.

are not from *suth tun*, 'the southern farmstead', but from *suth dun*, or 'southern hill'. Bone Acre Copse lacks any written record to confirm, but must be where bones were uncovered, either an earlier gravesite or perhaps a midden where animal bones had accumulated.

Boys Wood means 'wood wood', for the first element has nothing to do with young males but is from Old French *bois*, or 'wood'. Bell Bridge has no known link to the church, and hence perhaps this describes its 'humped or arched' shape. Farringdon Clump and Farringdon Copse are located near 'the fern covered hill' from which they take the name. Pert Copse may well come from a British *perth*, 'a hedge, bush'.

Remedy Gate features a brass tablet which is inscribed 'Beaneath this oak King Edward VI touched for the King's Evil'. Most often referred to as scrofula, it was any number of skin diseases affecting the lymph nodes of the neck and which was once considered curable simply by the 'touch' of the reigning monarch, although clearly from this it was also thought the touch could be passed on through an inanimate object. The word is from the Latin *scrofula* meaning 'brood sow'.

WINFRITH NEWBURGH

A name found in Domesday as Winfrode, this name comes from the Celtic river name *winn-frud*, or 'the white or bright stream'. The addition is from the name of the Newburgh family, here in the twelfth century.

Local names include Broomhill Farm, where the early forms are conflicting. The most likely explanation here is 'the hill where broom grows', although the first element has been confused with *breme*, 'bramble', and the second seen as *myln*, 'mill'. East Knighton is derived from *east cnihta tun* and describes 'the eastern farm of the young men', with the addition to differentiate from West Knighton, which no longer appears on the map.

Marley Bottom, Marley Pond and Marley Wood share Old English *myrge leah* and describe 'the woodland clearing where there was merry-making'. Coalhill Drove refers to 'the hill where charcoal was burnt', the addition speaking of the route regularly taken by herdsmen or drovers. Giddy Green may be from a surname; however, no record exists and thus it could be a reference to someone who once lived here, not particularly complimentary either for this is from *gydig* meaning 'mad, foolish'. Portway marks the 'way to the market town'; Randalls Farm was home to Richard Randall in 1664; Vines Down Buildings was associated with Margaret Vyne in 1682; and Withy Bed is from 'the withy or willowy plantation'.

WINTERBORNE CAME

The first of several place names which feature the name of 'the river which flows most strongly in winter', from Old English *winter-burna*. Here the name is recorded as Wintreburne in 1086 and as Winterburn Caam in 1280, and this addition refers to this place being held by the Norman Abbey at Caen.

Winterborne Faringdon has identical origins to the previous name, although this time the family is that of Thomas Faryngdon who were here around the middle of the fifteenth century. The name of Cripton has been used for a Barn, a Spinney and a Wood. Early records would point to Middle English *cribbe* with Old English *tun* and refer to 'the manger farmstead', which is probably telling us it was a cattle farm.

WINTERBORNE CLENSTON

Found as Wintreburne in 1086 and as Wynterburn Clencheston in 1303, this name comes from Old English *winter-burna*, 'the river which flows most strongly in winter', and takes its additions from 'the *tun* or farmstead of the Clench family'.

Here we find Charity Wood, referring to Williams' Charity, a bequest by the Williams family to provide an annual sum to be disposed of to the poor through the church. Clenstone Farm was also a part of this bequest, which must be a Saxon personal name with the common Old English *tun*.

WINTERBORNE HERRINGSTON

Again this is 'the strong winter river', here with a manorial addition first seen in the fourteenth century, referring to the family of Philip Hareng. There is also a record of this being the manor of the Beuchamp family in the thirteenth century, and indeed there is a record of the place being known as Wynterburn Beuchamp in 1243.

WINTERBORNE HOUGHTON

Records of Wintreburne in 1086 and Winterborn Huetone 1246 show this 'river that is stongest in winter' has taken the name of a second manor known as 'Hugh's estate', likely a reference to Hugh de Boscherbert who held this manor between the eventful year of 1066 but was absent (presumed dead) by the time of the Domesday survey in 1086.

There are other manorial references for Winterborne, any of which could easily have become the modern addition. In 1208, the name is seen as Winterburn Fercles, and records of Hugh, Thomas and Geoffrey de Fercles are all found around this time. The record from 1242 as Winterborn Moyun shows this place was associated with a family represented by John Mohun in 1278, with later records of Reginald and Roger de Mayun.

Here is the name of Cole Combe, with no surviving records prior to 1603. These forms are rather late and, while the second element is undoubtedly *cumb*, or 'valley', the first is difficult to tie down. Indeed this could be *col*, 'charcoal', *col*, 'cool', *cal*, 'cabbage', or the Saxon personal name Cola. Without earlier records it is impossible to know which is more likely.

Bully Plantation and Bully Wood share the common Old English *bula gehaeg*, 'the enclosure for bulls'; Dogshole Cottages may be *dogga hol*, 'the dog's hollow', but it seems more likely to be a personal name; Dunbury Lane is associated with 'the barrow on the hill'; Meriden is either from *more denu*, 'the moorland above the valley', or *mere denu*, 'the valley of the mares'; Shitley refers to 'the woodland clearing with a stream used as a sewer'; and the Stubbs takes its name from Old English *stubb*, or 'the tree stumps'.

WINTERBORNE KINGSTON

Found as Wintreburne in 1086, as Kingeswinterburn in 1194, and as Wyntrebrun Kyngeston in 1316, here is another example of 'the strong winter river'. Here the addition is clearly referring to this being a royal manor, held by the king from at least the reign of King John in the early thirteenth century.

Within this parish is Winterborne Muston, and here the addition comes from the family of Walter de Musters. Nutley Clump is named from *hnutu leah*, or the 'nut wood'.

WINTERBORNE MONKTON

This 'strong winter river' was under the control of the Cluniac priory of Le Wast, near Boulogne from the early thirteenth century. Thus the addition here refers to 'the farmstead of the monks'.

WINTERBORNE STEEPLETON

Here the 'strong river in winter' is overshadowed by the church steeple, as the name indicates. The earliest surviving records of this name are as Stipelwinterburn in 1199 and Wynterburn Stupilton in 1260.

WINTERBOURNE ST MARTIN

A place named for the 'strong winter river', which takes the dedication of the local church for distinction.

Ashton Farm already described 'the ash tree farmstead' before the addition of 'Farm'. Rew Hill is derived from 'the row of trees (or houses)'; Ballarat House takes its name from the town of Ballarat in Australia, itself thought to represent an Aboriginal tongue meaning 'resting place'; and Maiden Castle suggests this is impregnable, one which has never been taken.

WINTERBORNE STICKLAND

Another 'the strong winter river', with an addition from Old English sticol-lane, 'the steep lane'. This place is recorded as Winterburne in 1086 and as Winterburn Stikellane in 1203.

Quarelston Farm derives its name from the family of William Quarel, who was here by 1232. Canada is a transferred name, cannot accurately be described as a remoteness name, that part of the parish most distant from its centre, and must have come here for other, unknown, reasons. Normandy Farm, and from it Normandy Lodge, is probably from this place being held by the Norman abbey of Coutances at the time of the Domesday survey in 1086. Lastly, from Old English *ruh beorg* comes Rowbarrow, a name meaning 'the rough barrow'.

WINTERBORNE TOMSON

Found as simply Winterburne in 942, this 'strong winter river' is first recorded with the addition in 1268 as Wynterborn Thamston. This must be a manorial reference to a Thomas, although this person has not been recorded and his presence here was probably short lived. It is rather surprising to find this addition remaining when the Hussey family were lords of this manor for many years.

Den Wood comes from *denu* telling us it is 'the wood in the valley', although there is a record from 1284 listing this place as Denwodforlange, which also features the element *furlang*, or 'furlong'. This probably refers to a field or cultivated land standing alongside Den Wood. It should not be taken as being exactly one furlong in length, as this imperial measurement of 220 yards began life as simply the distance a plough team could turn with the plough before requiring a rest. Clearly, the distance would depend on the quality of the soil, the efficiency of the ploughshare, and the strength of the oxen and ploughman.

WINTERBORNE WHITECHURCH

Listed as Wintreburne in 1086 and as Wynterborn Wytecherch in 1268, here is another 'river stongest in winter' and with the additional 'white, or stone church' from Old English *hwit-cirice*.

La Lee Farm is an odd name, a clue to its origins seen with nearby Lee Wood. The wood clearing comes from Old English *leah* and referring to the 'woodland clearing', rather than the wood itself. Thus the name of La Lee Farm has identical origins, but has been influenced by the French definite article *la* and thus a name that cannot have existed prior to the Norman Conquest. Whatcombe Farm is from Old English *waet cumb*, thus describing 'the wet valley'.

Dolway Cottages is a name derived from *dal weg*, 'the way by the shared land'; Holloway's Wood has acquired a misleading possessive 's', the name simply speaks of 'the hollow way' — that is, the hollow worn away over a long period of time; Scent Close Plantation is from Old English *senget* and tells us of 'the place cleared by burning', which not only cleared the natural growth but provided a good source of nutrients in the form of the ash.

WINTERBORNE ZELSTON

Listed as Wintreborne in 1086 and Wynterbourn Selyston in 1350, here is 'the strong winter river' which was 'the *tun* or farmstead of the Seles family' by the fourteenth century.

Locally we find Huish, a name describing 'the area of land which would support a family'; while Bushes Barn and Bushes Pit are unlikely to refer to a shrub but to a family name; Speaks comes from the Speke family, who were farming here by the eighteenth century; and Vermin Lane features a word still in use today, although vermin was originally used to refer to any noxious or offensive creature.

WINTERBOURNE ABBAS

Here is a name that tells us it was 'the river which flows more strongly in winter and which belongs to the abbey of Cerne'. The name comes from Old English *winter-burna* and Latin *abbatis* and is listed as Wintreburne in 1086 and as Wynterburn Abbattis in 1244.

WINTON

A very modern name and one which cannot have been seen before 1859, for that was when the Earl of Eglinton was created Earl of Winton. He was a relative of the Talbot sisters (see Talbot Village).

WITCHAMPTON

Listed in Domesday as Wichemetune in 1086, this name comes from Old English *wic haeme tun* and telling us of 'the farmstead of those who dwell on the site of the Romano-British settlement'.

Dean Farm tells us, from Old English *denu*, that it lies 'in the valley'. East Hemsworth and West Hemsworth share a common origin in 'Hemmede's enclosure'. Abbey Buildings and Abbey House take their names from Abbey Barn, which, according to tradition, was once used as a chapel. Cutler's Coppice reminds us of the family of John Cutler, here by 1664; Haggates Cottages also must have taken a surname, although no record of such a family has survived to the present day; Zannies Coppice and Zannies Cottages are also taken from a surname, and the place is listed as Sannys in 1811; new Town was a planned eighteenth-century development to rehouse those displaced from More Crichel; and Wall's Cottages were built near the site of the Roman villa at Hemsworth.

WOODLANDS

A name not found before 1244, when it appeared as Wodelande. This comes from Old English *wudu land* and describes 'the cultivated land of or by the wood'.

Bagman's Copse has identical origins to the lost place name of Baggeridge and describes 'the bag-shaped copse'. Charlton Dairy Farm was 'the farmstead of the peasants'; Knowle Hill describes 'the hillock'; the 'farmstead of the hillock' is now recorded as Knowlton; Matterley Cottages describes 'the woodland clearing around the maple trees'; Bolehays Copse is named from 'the bull's enclosure'; David's Cross is where several lanes meet, a crossroads; and Stepping Stones marks where the stream has been crossed since at least the nineteenth century.

Monmouth's Ash is named after the Duke of Monmouth who was hiding in an ash tree near here after the Battle of Sedgemoor on 6 July 1685. The tree itself is no longer standing. This was the final and decisive battle of the Monmouth Rebellion, resulting in some 500 men being tried at the Bloody Assizes, many being transported and some executed by drawing and quartering.

WOODSFORD

Not quite as predictable as it may seem, for the first element is not *wudu* but a personal name. Listed as Wardesford in 1086, this comes from 'the ford of a man called Weard', the suffix is clearly Old English *ford*.

Locally we find Sturt's Weir, a name derived from former resident Humphrey Sturt, who lived at East Woodford Farm by 1774. The remains of Woodsford Castle still show some of the rooms. Names such as the King's Room, the Queen's Room, the Guard Chamber, North Hall, and South Hall are of obvious origins, and the Beacon Tower housed a light said to have been lit every night to guide travellers through the ford.

WOODYATES (EAST & WEST)

Found as Wdegeate in the ninth century and as Odiete in Domesday, this name comes from Old English *wudu geat* and speaks of 'the gate or gap of the wood'. The additions, fairly recent developments, are self-explanatory.

At West Woodyates is Denbose Wood, a surname with records of a number of representatives including Philip Denebaud, William Denebaud, and John Denebaude in the thirteenth and fourteenth centuries. Pill Ash has two potential Old English origins, *pil* would refer to 'the ash tree near the shaft' and *pyll* 'the small stream by the ash trees'.

Fingerpost at Lane End.

WOOL

Found in Domesday as Welle, this name comes from Old English *wiella* and describes this as the '(place at) the springs or streams'.

Bindon Abbey comes from Old English *binnan dun*, or the '(place) within the hill'. This is not an accurate description of this place; the name has been transferred from the original Cistercian abbey at Little Bindon near Bindon Hill. Bovington speaks of 'the farmstead associated with a man called Bofa'; records show the name of Woodstreet Farm became corrupted after the thirteenth century, earlier this was from *wind steort*, 'a winding tongue of land'; Colliers Lane and Collier's Barn share a common origin in *coliere*, a 'maker or seller of charcoal'; Moncton Bushes grew at 'the farm belonging to the monks'; Little Perry Coppice was the 'smaller pear tree coppice'; Pug Pit was considered 'haunted by a goblin'; and Fair Ford, said to be named from the Dog-Fair, when boys ran through the streets with a whip, driving away any dog wandering the streets which they considered fair game.

It should be noted that the vast majority of pubs named the Ship Inn, especially those inland, have nothing to do with ships but a corruption of *sceap*, or 'sheep'. Ironically, at Wool the reverse is the case and this pub actually refers to the nearby ocean.

WOOLLAND

Records of this name include Wormonde in 934 and Winlande in 1086. This name comes from Old English *wynn land* and refers to 'the estate with pasture'.

Broad Aldermore, Long Aldermore, Chitcombe Aldermoor and Swandhill Aldermore share a name that is derived from *alor mor*, or 'the moorland by the alder trees'. The additions refer to 'Cytta's valley', in the case of Chitmore, a family name, in the case of Swandhill, while the difference between Broad and Long relates to their early situation along the main road, the latter spread along it and the former aligned leading away from it.

WOOTTON FITZPAINE

From Old English *wudu tun*, the basic name means 'the farmstead at or of the wood'. The name is recorded as Wodetone in 1086 and as Wotton Fitz Payn in 1392, and the addition refers to the Fitz Payn family who were here by the fourteenth century.

WOOTTON GLANVILLE

Found as Widtone in Domesday, as Wotton in 1268, Wotton Clauyle in 1280, Wolfrenewotton in 1303, and Woutton Glaunvylle in 1344, this name shares its basic name with the previous entry and is again 'the farmstead at or of the wood'. Here the addition is a reminder that the Glanville family held this manor, beginning with Geoffrey de Glaunvile in 1258 and Mabel de Glamuill ten years later. This surname comes from another place name, Glanville in Normandy, which itself comes from a Germanic personal name and Old French *ville* describing 'Glando's farm'.

Local names include Blackmore Cottages and Blackmore Ford Bridge, both derived from 'the dark moor'; Osehill Green was once 'Osweald's hill'; Basket's Farm was worked by Thomas Basket; Buttons Coppice was associated with William Budden in 1664; Dunning's Lane refers to the home of John Dunnyng; and the oddly named trees known as Gog and Magog, names recorded in a number of ancient books where they are most often named as giants (although some suggest thay they are men, demons, and even nations).

Harbin's Farm was home to William Harbyn in 1546; Loader's Hill Farm supported the Loder family who were owners of the manor of Osehill in the early eighteenth century; Mullett's Coppice reminds us of Ralph Mulett, here in 1664; and Round Chimneys Farm is named from the mansion house that once stood here and that did not have the rectangular chimneys seen elsewhere.

WORTH MATRAVERS

This Old English *worth*, or 'enclosure', has the addition from the Mautravers family, who were here from the fourteenth century. The name is recorded as simply Wirde in Domesday and as Worth Matrauers in 1664.

Local names include Caplestone, which comes from 'Cabel's farmstead'; Quarre can still be seen as 'the quarry'; Renscombe Farm started life as 'the raven's valley', or perhaps this is used as a personal name and 'Hremn's valley'; Seacombe Bottom is easy to understand as meaning 'the valley opening out to the sea'; while Black Man's Rock remembers the body of a Lascar seaman washed up on this rock, a presumed victim from the nearby wreck a day or two previously, the term Lascar referring specifically to those from the Indian subcontinent who served on merchant vessels between the sixteenth and nineteenth centuries. Buttery Corner refers to a shelf created by quarrying and would appear to be saying this was a 'liquor store' and almost certainly alluding to smuggling. Gallows Gore Cottages marks the point where a number of tracks converge and was where three men from Swanage were hung, drawn and quartered for their part in the Duke of Monmouth's rebellion in 1685.

Cottages and Woodhyde Farm are found where what was once 'the widow's hide of land', not actually a measurement but a piece of land that would support a family for a year. While we have no idea of the area of land, we do know that the widow in question was Hawise de Baschelville, wife of the late Hugh Fitz Grip, who held 116 hides of land in the county at the time of the Domesday survey.

Chapman's Pool is either a somewhat corrupted form of 'Sceortmann's pool', or is from Old English *sceort maennes* meaning 'the short community pool' and possibly the bay where they bathed together with the neighbouring parish of Corfe Castle.

The Square & Compass is a tradesman's sign, the tools used by craftsmen, such as carpenters, joiners and stonemasons.

WRAXALL

Derived from Old English *wrocc halh* and telling us of 'the nook of land frequented by the buzzard or similar bird of prey', this name is found as Brocheshale in 1086 and as Wrokeshal in 1196.

WYKE REGIS

An ancient royal manor, hence the addition, this name is found as Wike in 984 and as Kingeswik in 1242. Here is Old English *wic* together with 'the specialised farm of the king'.

Bridge Farm is near the river crossing to Portland, an obvious crossing point that is known as Small Mouth and is the narrow point here. Little Francis takes its name from Middle English *fraunchise*, clearly related to modern 'franchise' and here referring to the sphere of influence of local government. Marquis Terrace is named for the Marquis of Granby, not resident here but in nearby Chickerell. Cacique was a word used in the Caribbean nations to describe a native chieftain or leader, and here Cacique is the name of a house, probably brought back by someone who worked or traded there.

Pubs here include the Wyke Smugglers, a name that needs no explanation, while the Albert Inn, named for the consort of Queen Victoria, may not be quite so obvious.

WYNFORD EAGLE

A name found in Domesday as Wenfrot and which by 1288 had become Wynfrod Egle. This is a Celtic river name from *winn frud* meaning 'the white or bright stream'. The addition refers to the del Egle family, here in the thirteenth century.

YETMINSTER

A name recorded as Etiminstre in 1086, this name comes from a Saxon personal name and Old English *mynster* and tells us it was 'the church of a man called Eata'.

Chapter 21

Common Place Name Elements

ELEMENT	ORIGIN	MEANING
ac	Old English	oak tree
banke	Old Scandinavian	bank, hill slope
bearu	Old English	grove, wood
bekkr	Old Scandinavian	stream
berg	Old Scandinavian	hill
birce	Old English	birch tree
brad	Old English	broad
broc	Old English	brook, stream
brycg	Old English	bridge
burh	Old English	fortified place
burna	Old English	stream
by	Old Scandinavian	farmstead
ceap	Old English	market
ceaster	Old English	Roman stronghold
cirice	Old English	church
clif	Old English	cliff, slope
cocc	Old English	woodcock
cot	Old English	cottage
cumb	Old English	valley
cweorn	Old English	queorn
cyning	Old English	king
dael	Old English	valley
dalr	Old Scandinavian	valley
denu	Old English	valley
draeg	Old English	portage
dun	Old English	hill
ea	Old English	river
east	Old English	east
ecg	Old English	edge
eg	Old English	island

ELEMENT	ORIGIN	MEANING
eorl	Old English	nobleman
eowestre	Old English	fold for sheep
fald	Old English	animal enclosure
feld	Old English	open land
ford	Old English	river crossing
ful	Old English	foul, dirty
geard	Old English	yard
geat	Old English	gap, pass
haeg	Old English	enclosure
haeth	Old English	heath
haga	Old English	hedged enclosure
halh	Old English	nook of land
ham	Old English	homestead
hamm	Old English	river meadow
heah	Old English	high, chief
hlaw	Old English	tumulus, mound
hoh	Old English	hill spur
hop	Old English	enclosed valley
hrycg	Old English	ridge
hwaete	Old English	wheat
hwit	Old English	white
hyll	Old English	hill
lacu	Old English	streamlet, water course
lang	Old English	long
langr	Old Scandinavian	long
leah	Old English	woodland clearing
lytel	Old English	little
meos	Old English	moss
mere	Old English	lake
middle	Old English	middle
mor	Old English	moorland
myln	Old English	mill
niwe	Old English	new
north	Old English	north
ofer	Old English	bank, ridge
penn	Old English	rocky hill
pol	Old English	pool, pond
preost	Old English	priest

ELEMENT	ORIGIN	MEANING
ruh	Old English	rough
salh	Old English	willow
sceaga	Old English	small wood, copse
sceap	Old English	sheep
stan	Old English	stone, boundary stone
steinn	Old Scandinavian	stone, boundary stone
stapol	Old English	post, pillar
stoc	Old English	secondary or special settlement
stocc	Old English	stump, log
stow	Old English	assembly or holy place
straet	Old English	Roman road
suth	Old English	south
torr	Old English	rock hill or outcrop
thorp	Old Scandinavian	outlying farmstead
treow	Old English	tree, post
tun	Old English	farmstead
wald	Old English	woodland, forest
wella	Old English	spring, stream
west	Old English	west
wic	Old English	specialised, usually dairy farm
withig	Old English	willow tree
worth	Old English	an enclosure
wudu	Old English	wood

Chapter 24
Bibliography

The Place Names of Dorset Parts I, II and III by A D Mills
Melbury Abbas by Bob Breach
Sherbourne Observed by Gerald Pitman
Shaftesbury (An Illustrated History) by Brenda Innes
Explore Christchurch by Keith Jarvis
Cerne's Giant and Village Guide by Rodney Legg
The Makers of Christchurch: A Thousand Year History by Michael Stannerd

Also available from Amberley Publishing

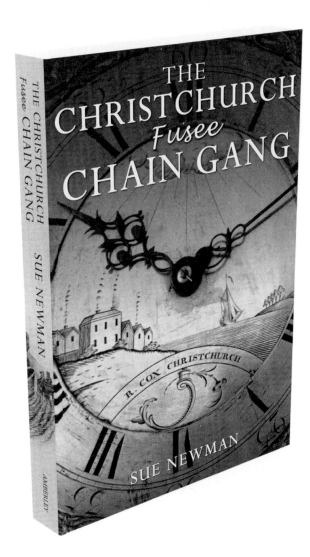

*The Christchurch
Fusee Chain Gang*

Sue Newman

ISBN: 978-1-84868-441-6

Price: £16.99

Available from all good bookshops, or order direct
from our website www.amberleybooks.com

Also available from Amberley Publishing

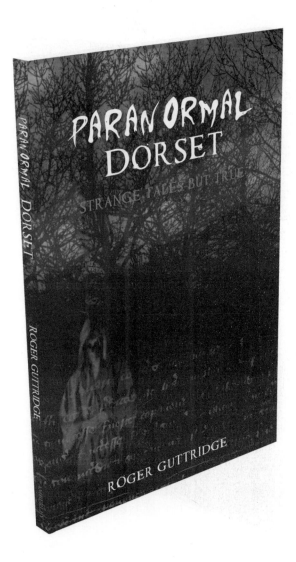

Paranormal Dorset
Roger Guttridge
ISBN: 978-1-84868-394-5
Price: £12.99

Available from all good bookshops, or order direct
from our website www.amberleybooks.com

Also available from Amberley Publishing

*Dorset Pubs
and Breweries*

Tim Edgell

ISBN: 978-1-84868-203-0

Price: £12.99

Available from all good bookshops, or order direct
from our website www.amberleybooks.com

Also available from Amberley Publishing

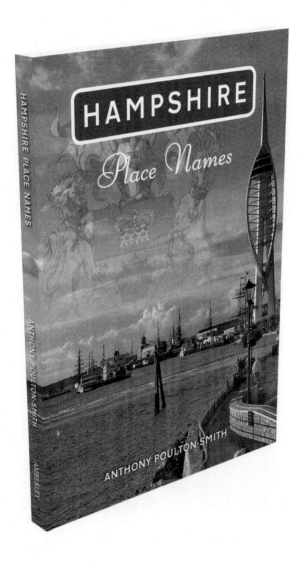